ᴛʜᴇ LOOPING
HANDBOOK

Teachers and
Students
Progressing
Together

ALSO BY JIM GRANT, BOB JOHNSON AND IRV RICHARDSON

Our Best Advice:
The Multiage Problem Solving Handbook

Multiage Q&A:
101 Practical Answers to Your Most Pressing Questions

ALSO BY JIM GRANT AND BOB JOHNSON

A Common Sense Guide to Multiage Practices

ALSO BY JIM GRANT AND IRV RICHARDSON

The Multiage Handbook:
A Comprehensive Resource for Multiage Practices

ALSO BY JIM GRANT

The Looping Classroom: Teachers and Students Progressing
Together. (Videos: Teacher/Administrator Version and
Parent Version)

Developmental Education in the 1990's

"I Hate School!"

Worth Repeating: Giving Children
a Second Chance at School Success

THE LOOPING HANDBOOK

Teachers and Students Progressing Together

Written by: Jim Grant
Bob Johnson
Irv Richardson

Edited by Aldene Fredenburg

Crystal Springs Books, Peterborough, New Hampshire

Printed in the United States of America

Published by Crystal Springs Books
Ten Sharon Road
PO Box 500
Peterborough, New Hampshire 03458
1-800-321-0401

Publisher Cataloging-in-Publication Data

Grant, Jim, 1942-
     The looping handbook / written by Jim Grant, Bob
Johnson, Irv Richardson.—1st ed.
[176]p. : cm.
Includes bibliography and index.

Summary : Looping is a practice where a teacher moves with her class from one grade to the next, while the teacher previously teaching the higher class cycles back to pick up a new class. Provides a multiyear relationship between teacher and child.

ISBN 1-884548-07-5
1. Teaching. 2. Learning. 3. Nongraded schools. 4. Team learning approach in education. I. Johnson, Bob, 1942- . II. Richardson, Irv, 1956- . III. Title.
371.302' 82—dc20   1996   CIP
LC Card Number: 96-83277

To Bob McQuillen, my high school shop teacher for three years, and my friend for forty. He reached out to all students, including hard-to-reach kids, and has probably saved more at-risk kids than any other teacher in our school system.

Bob taught me practical skills which allowed me to pursue my lifelong avocations of house and antique automobile restoration, and gave me the confidence I needed to aspire to greater things. He gave me extra time, and extra attention, when I needed it, and the path I have taken since reflects the benefits of his care and concern.

— Jim Grant

To Helen Witty, a special teacher and friend who within the field of special education has devoted her life to providing consistency and stable routine throughout the multiple years of each student's school experience.

— Bob Johnson

To Bill Richards, an extraordinary teacher. I was privileged to have many different classes and experiences with Bill during my years in high school. Bill helped me understand the power of teaching and the joy of watching others grow.

He always had time to listen and to help me grow. For me, Bill was an outstanding teacher and mentor, and he remains a good friend.

— Irv Richardson

To Philip Pratt, my high school science teacher. His easygoing manner belied a concern for the environment and an understanding of social issues that were ahead of his time. It took me years to realize that much of what I believe and know to be true about the world came from Mr. Pratt.

— Aldene Fredenburg

ACKNOWLEDGMENTS

We would like to thank the many people who contributed to the creation of this book. They are:

Char Forsten, former multiyear/multiage teacher and principal from Dublin Consolidated School in Dublin, New Hampshire, for offering her insights to the authors, and for contributing summer project ideas to the "Summer Learning" chapter of this book;

Jan Jubert, first and second grade looping teacher from Lac du Flambeau Public School in Lac du Flambeau, Wisconsin, for providing information about her classroom and for allowing us to reprint information on her summer transition program and excerpts from her parent handbook (including an extensive outline of her first and second grade looping curriculum);

Karen Rettig, first and second grade looping teacher in Liberty Center Elementary School in Liberty Center, Ohio, who shared her process in setting up her looping class and her way of communicating with her group of parents. She also provided two calendars of summer activities for our "Summer Learning" chapter and shared with us the results of a parent survey taken at her school.

Teachers Rebecca Moyer and Pam Clem, parent Sheila Green, and students Michael Combs and Brandon Green, of Ashby Lee Elementary School in Quicksburg, Virginia, for sharing their experiences with looping;

Gretchen Goodman, for her excerpt on spotting possible learning difficulties, from her contribution to the book, *Our Best Advice: The Multiage Problem Solving Handbook;*

Yvette Zgonc, a nationally-known lecturer on cooperative discipline and ADD/ADHD, who provided valuable information on dealing with difficult students;

Esther Wright, well-known lecturer and author of several books, who allowed us to reprint a portion of her book, *Loving Discipline A to Z;*

Stephen Parker, a personal consultant in New England and New York, who spoke at length about his own experience as a student in a multiyear arrangement in the late 1950s and early 1960s;

Daniel L. Burke and *Phi Delta Kappan* Magazine, for allowing us to reprint Mr. Burke's article, "Multi-Year Teacher/Student Relationships Are a Long-Overdue Arrangement;"

Teaching K-8 Magazine, for allowing us to reprint the article, "Twice the Learning and Twice the Love," by Deborah Jacoby; and

The Carnegie Foundation for the Advancement of Teaching, for allowing us to excerpt the late Dr. Ernest L. Boyer's book, *The Basic School: A Community for Learning.*

A special thanks goes to the dedicated people of the Attleboro, Massachusetts, School District, who welcomed us into their schools and showed us the phenomenal power that looping, or the multiyear assignment, has on children's lives. They are:

Dr. Joseph Rappa, superintendent of schools, a dynamic individual who has used the authority of his position to spearhead the creation of a truly child-centered educational system;

Theodore (Ted) Thibodeau, assistant superintendent, who spent a whole day introducing SDE to the Attleboro system, and who showed a consistent ability to put the teachers and students at ease in sharing their concerns and ideas with him;

Frank Leary, principal, and Lynne Marcet and Kristin Manning, fifth-sixth grade teachers, at Cyril K. Brennan Middle School;

Kenneth Cabral, principal, and Glenn Killough, third-fourth grade teacher, at Joseph Finberg Elementary School; and the students in Glenn Killough's fourth-grade class;

Dolores Fitzgerald, principal, and third-fourth grade teachers Cindy Edwards, Phyllis Sisson, Lisa Hopkins, and Connie O'Riley, and student teacher Kim Tobin, at A. Irvin Studley Elementary School; and

Mimi Forbes, principal, and Dave Cox, seventh-eighth grade teacher, at Robert J. Coelho Middle School; and Dave Cox's eighth-grade students: Jason Caine, Paulina Czerwonka, Alison Frenier, John Gagne, and Brian Sullivan.

We would also like to thank Robert Lincoln, the principal of Tolland Middle School in Tolland, Connecticut, for describing the Attleboro school system in such glowing terms that we had to go see for ourselves.

At The Society For Developmental Education and Crystal Springs Books, we would like to thank:

Susan Dunholter, who created a clean, crisp, attractive design for this book;

Lorraine Walker, publishing manager, who with her constant attention and down-to-earth pragmatism helped keep this book on track;

Lillian Grant, who typed parts of this book, then read the completed work with a critical eye to detail;

Laura Taylor, who typeset many of the more graphically complex elements of this book; and

Christine Landry, whose expertise in book composition allowed her to fine-tune our efforts into a finished project.

Finally, a note about editor and wordsmith Aldene Fredenburg, who went beyond her scope as editor in gathering information from phone and on-site interviews, to collect real-world experiences on the part of looping practitioners. She worked on this book with a sense of mission and the fervor of an advocate of multiyear teaching.

CONTENTS

For years we've been listening to teachers bewail the fact that they needed "just a little more time" with certain students; they ran out of school year just as some children were ready to make a breakthrough. This book, *The Looping Handbook,* presents a solution to that problem — a solution so easy to implement that it is available to virtually every school in the country, at every level. It's probably also the one reform in which teachers, administrators and parents are instantly on the same side.

Looping — the practice of allowing teachers to keep the same students over a two-year period (sometimes longer) — provides teachers and students at least a month of extra instructional time by eliminating the "getting-to-know-you" period at the beginning of the second year of a looping class. Students pick up where they left off, both instructionally and socially, and get into the swing of school in moments, rather than weeks.

Looping has been tried in varying degrees around the country. Some schools may have only one looping classroom, initiated by a pair of teachers who talked their principal into letting them give it a try. Other school systems have gone into it in a more formalized way, by presenting the concept to the school board and the public and presenting looping options at every grade level.

This book presents the benefits of looping, and provides profiles of a number of looping classes of different grade levels. The book also discusses parent input and parent relations, as well as potential problems with looping and possible solutions to these problems.

Probably the best source of information about looping is someone who has experienced it; therefore, we've provided addresses, phone numbers and FAX numbers of teachers and principals of schools who practice looping, and who've agreed to welcome questions about their programs, as well as visitors. (If you plan to visit a looping program, call first. Not only is it courteous — and in most instances required — but you will have a more productive visit if you give the school some advance notice.)

The Society For Developmental Education has been instrumental in spreading the word about looping around the country via its conferences, workshops and seminars. It plans to continue and expand its work on this most important reform. For information about seminars on looping and other related topics, contact:

The Society For Developmental Education
Ten Sharon Road
PO Box 577
Peterborough NH 03458
1-800-924-9621

THE LOOPING HANDBOOK

Teachers and Students Progressing Together

CHAPTER 1

The Multiyear Classroom
A Stable Force in Children's Lives

Our experience indicates that the most important variable in a positive elementary school program is the constant attention of a single teacher/caregiver with whom the child can develop a predictable and meaningful relationship. As children reach the ages of eleven and twelve, peers become more important and teachers less important to children.

But especially in these first stages of independence, children need one teacher there as an anchor, as well as an object for rebellion.

— Chip Wood, *Yardsticks*

What is Looping?

Looping is a pretty simple concept. A teacher decides that, instead of spending one year with a class of children, she wants to spend two, or sometimes three, so she talks the teacher in the next grade into dropping back to her present grade level, and moves to the next grade along with her kids. It's a relatively inexpensive, easy reform.

But why does it work so well? According to Dr. Joseph Rappa, superintendent of the Attleboro, Massachusetts, school district (which provides multiyear assignments to all of its first- through eighth-grade students with all of its 400 teachers),

> Student attendance in grades 2 through 8 has been increased from 92 percent average daily attendance (ADA) to 97.2 percent ADA. Retention rates have decreased by over 43 percent in those same grades. Discipline and suspensions, especially at the middle schools (grades 5 through 8), have declined significantly. Special education referrals have decreased by over 55 percent, and staff attendance has improved markedly from an average of seven days absent per staff member per year, to less than three. (Rappa 1993)

Most teachers, when talking about looping, mention time as a factor: a month of learning time built into the second and sometimes third year at the beginning of school, another month built into the end of the first year, as students end the year on a high note. But time is a tool, to be used with other child-friendly strategies, to promote what is at the core of looping — relationship.

On Michael Combs — and the Looping Model

Michael entered first grade having multiple disabilities with a full-time aide. We worked closely with the resource teacher and aide in developing a daily contract for appropriate behavior. Our goal was to provide a secure and stable environment in which Michael would require the services of an aide only half a day at the end of first grade. Michael adapted gradually to the routines, and by the beginning of second grade met our goal of a half day with the aide. Since the first grade class looped to second grade with the same teacher and classmates, Michael adjusted well to second grade. By the end of second grade an aide was no longer needed. He began third grade with a new teacher, no aide, and new classmates. Presently, he is functioning well and with no special education services and is looking forward to fourth grade. We believe the looping model enabled Michael to function academically and socially during a difficult adjustment period in his life.

Pam Clem, Teacher
First and Second Grades

Ashby Lee Elementary School
Quicksburg, Virginia

Relationship — that of teacher to student, to the parents, to other teachers, and to the curriculum — is what gives looping its power. Given time, a teacher can:

- develop a deeper understanding of students' learning styles and needs, both academic and emotional.
- better understand students' family dynamics and the parents' needs and expectations regarding their children's education.
- approach the curriculum in more depth, knowing that there is more time to help students make connections in their learning.
- understand the requirements of the teachers coming before and after, and develop a more all-encompassing view of the educational process through which her students will pass.

Looping has gotten a lot of press coverage lately, and within the past year there's been a groundswell of interest in it; but it's not a new concept. Rudolf Steiner, an Austrian educator and philosopher, founded the Waldorf Schools in the early 1900s in order to educate the children of domestics who worked for the Waldorf Astoria cigarette factory in Stuttgart, Germany. Waldorf schools still follow his precepts to this day; a Waldorf teacher stays with a group of students from first through eighth grade.

In Germany, children are grouped heterogeneously and stay with the same teacher from grades one through four; Japan and Israel also have multiyear "family groupings" in the lower grades, and multiyear teacher-student relationships by content area in their secondary schools. For instance, a secondary math teacher will teach the same students algebra, geometry and other content areas, while the science teacher will teach life sciences, chemistry and physics.

In the United States, although multiyear education hasn't been the norm for over 150 years, teachers have been quietly practicing "teacher rotation" for years. (see page 17).

Easy to Implement

Although some schools approach looping very formally, setting up committees, visiting other schools, and seeking parent and school board approval before adopting a multiyear configuration, it's actually about the easiest school reform to implement. Since most school principals have the authority to reassign teachers within their schools by simply notifying the school board and the superintendent, all it really takes to begin looping is two teachers willing to try the concept and an understanding principal willing to give them the nod.

The cost of implementing looping is minimal, usually limited to some new instructional materials and supplies for the teachers and perhaps some staff development funds to help them get up to speed on their new curriculums. Extensive training is not necessary; any experienced teacher will already have most of the skills necessary to succeed in a looping classroom.

TEACHER ROTATION

"Shall teachers in city graded schools be advanced from grade to grade with their pupils through a series of two, three, four or more years, so that they may come to know the children they teach and be able to build the work of the latter years on that of the earlier years, or shall teachers be required to remain year after year in the same grade while the children, promoted from grade to grade, are taught by a different teacher each year? This I believe to be one of the most important questions of city school administration."

"To this plan two objections are frequently raised: (1) that the teacher may be inefficient, and that no group of children should be condemned to the care and instruction of an inefficient teacher through a series of years; (2) that the full influence of the personality of any one teacher has been exhausted by the end of a year, and children should therefore come in contact with a new personality each year. The answer to both objections is easy and evident. The inefficient teacher should be eliminated. The man or woman who is unable to teach a group of children through more than one year should not be permitted to waste their money, time and opportunity through a single year."

"A personality which a child between the ages of 6 and 12 may exhaust in a year must be very shallow. What the child needs is not an everchanging personality, but a guide along the pathway of knowledge to the high road of life."

Looking at some advantages:

- There is a savings of time at the end of the first year of the cycle because with the exception of a few pupils who may be assigned elsewhere, the grouping process has taken care of itself.

- There is a savings of time at the beginning of the second year in which the teacher and pupils have worked together. The teacher understands the placement of each pupil in the curriculum and each pupil knows his classmates and the "ground rules" which operate within the class.

- Teacher Rotation emphasizes the importance of the teacher being a specialist in teaching children instead of being a specialist in a given subject area.

- Parents are better able to understand the school program because they know the teacher and understand her methods of working with children.

— Officer of Education
Department of Education, 1913

In contrast to other major reforms like year-round education and multiage education, looping doesn't require a long lead time, extensive planning, or substantial research. And because looping can be implemented quietly, in a low-key fashion, it won't as readily become a target of pressure groups opposed to school reform.

Parental support is an essential ingredient of any school reform. Luckily, looping is a concept embraced enthusiastically by most parents once they understand its benefits. (Parents have actually initiated some looping arrangements by saying to a favorite teacher, "You've given my child the best year he's ever had. I wish you could have him for another year!")

Few Potential Problems

Any education reform has problems, and looping has its share. Fortunately, the problems associated with looping are few, and most are avoided with a little planning (see "Look Before You Loop," page 105).

In brief, my son Brandon had a wonderful year in kindergarten. However, the transition from kindergarten to first grade was not so wonderful. Weeks before first grade, questions and concerns about his teacher, classmates, room location, etc., began to come from Brandon. The first two weeks of first grade were a real struggle for both Brandon and me, but thanks to a great teacher we survived.

Brandon was to be with the same teacher and class in the second grade. Knowing this through the summer, we had absolutely no anxiety when we began second grade. In fact, he was anxious to go back to school to see his teacher and friends. It was a very pleasant experience. To quote Brandon when he came home from school on the first day of second grade, "It was just like a family reunion." I just hope the rest of our school years can be as nice as this one has been.

Sheila Green, Parent
Brandon Green, Student

Ashby Lee Elementary School
Quicksburg, Virginia

Looping Versus Multiage

Many educators who have taught both multiage classes and single-grade, multiyear or "looping" classes say they prefer the latter. Char Forsten, former elementary school teacher and principal of Dublin Consolidated School of Dublin, New Hampshire, says,

> I've done multiage and looping; I prefer multiage to single-grade, single-year teaching, but I must admit looping is easier.
>
> With multiage there's always movement in and out of the class as a group of older students leaves and is replaced by a group of younger students. With looping in a single-grade class, the ability range and age range are less, and the class population stays the same except for occasional new kids moving in, and you can really get momentum.

Multiage education does have some advantages over looping; with the wider age range, there's more of an opportunity for children to "eavesdrop" on each other's learning, and older children get to act as positive role models and mentors for younger children. This role as the older, more knowledgeable student is perceived as very important, and children in a multiage class look forward to the time when they can be the veterans in the class.

Also, with the seamless, continuous progress curriculum possible in a multiage class, children can truly learn at their own rates, and may have the option of spending an additional year of learning time in a multiage class without the trauma of grade-level retention.

On the other hand, multiage programs take a lot more work and planning and a lot more energy than single-grade looping classes. A teacher thinking about multiage may want to try looping first, and either stay with the looping configuration or use it as a good solid first step to multiage education.

Not a lot has been written on looping, but a few good articles exist on the topic. We've included two here, and have referenced others in the bibliography.

"Twice the Learning and Twice the Love," by teacher Deborah Jacoby (see next page), is a narrative of her experiences with her first multiyear class. It is reprinted here with the permission of *Teaching K-8* Magazine. It provides a good personal look at many of the benefits of looping.

"Multi-Year Teacher/Student Relationships Are a Long-Overdue Arrangement," by Daniel L. Burke, a superintendent of an Antioch, Illinois school district, gives an overview of some of the multiyear programs in existence around the country (see page 21). The article is reprinted from the magazine, *Phi Delta Kappan*.

A teacher discovers the joys and sorrows of holding on and letting go as she moves with her students from first grade to second grade.

Twice the Learning and Twice the Love

by Deborah Jacoby

In September 1990, with freshly scrubbed faces, brand new clothes, and bulging backpacks full of newly purchased school supplies, 20 children tentatively crossed the portal of my first grade classroom. Some were holding an older sibling's hand or hiding behind the protective folds of their mother's skirt. One parent had a videocamera to record the momentous occasion.

Before saying goodbye, their mothers helped them find their names on their cubbies and hung up their jackets. After a quick kiss, a giant bear hug, or a smile and a wave that seemed to say, "I'll be okay, Mom," the new students quietly made their way to the tables to color or do puzzles and we began our year.

Gradually, we got to know and trust each other. We had a full year — hatching chicks, loose teeth, birthday treats and other significant first grade milestones. One by one, the first graders became more fluent readers and writers as typically happens at this age.

In the spring, my principal approached me about taking them on to second grade. I was hesitant about mastering new curriculum, wondering if I'd be able to continue to challenge and interest the same children in second grade. But knowing how much I enjoyed these children and excited about the prospect of doing something different, I agreed.

Back in the saddle

In September 1991, amidst a sea of moms, tears and all the trepidation of the first day of school, there were 20 confident second graders who rushed into my classroom and quickly began unpacking their supplies, chatting about summer vacations.

Last spring, the children made their own name labels for their desks and cubbies. There were no first day jitters. Instead, there were feelings of familiarity.

The startup that fall was different for me than in any other year. We jumped right into projects without any of the usual transition time. Behavioral expectations had been set the year before. I tried to make sure certain things about the routine were different, but found that the children preferred the comfort of the same routines.

The continuing curriculum

All year, curriculum was partially defined by my previous experiences with the children. I needed to do very little assessment of skills. I knew where we had left off in the spring. In fact, several children had unfinished stories from the end of first grade that they completed in second.

When we discussed books and authors, we would often compare or contrast a book to one we had read the previous year. I was able to build on known foundations and utilize the children's strengths and talents more than I was ever able to before.

Reprinted with permission of the publisher, Teaching K-8, from the October 1995 issue of *Teaching K-8* Magazine.

This was perhaps most true in reading and writing. I had watched my students' skills emerge and solidify. I was able to reinforce those skills in a style that was consistent over two years. For example, knowing the process we had used in researching chameleons in the fall of first grade and polar bears in the winter, I was able to build on those steps to plan for researching planets in the winter of second grade. Each project built on the last one.

By the second year, I was able to offer more constructive criticism on the students' academic work without damaging our relationship. They already knew that I believed in them and in their cognitive abilities and they trusted my instincts.

Strengthening the bond

The students' relationships with me and with each other deepened over time. We knew each other's strengths and weaknesses. And as a family, we shared triumphs and tears.

The whole class cheered when Tom finished a 500-piece puzzle. We were all saddened when Andrew's dog died and when Lindsay moved to California. Each time someone celebrated a birthday, the children dictated sentences for the birthday card that described why the birthday child was special. I was impressed by the precise insights the children offered about each other. The sense of the classroom being an interdependent community of learners was so very strong.

The two-year sequence benefited the shy, quiet children tremendously as well. There always seems to be one or two children who rarely talk in class, although their parents say that they are never quiet at home. Those children grew increasingly comfortable in the classroom, and by the middle of the second year, came fully out of their shells; as our time together increased, school simulated the comfort and intimacy of home and family.

A time to share

I was also able to develop trusting relationships with parents and families. Together, we charted their children's ups and downs over two years. The parents, children and I were able to reflect on growth and change over a greater time period. When Claire wrote an exceptional story that had rabbits as the theme, I was able to refer back to when she wrote a story about rabbits in first grade and point to specific elements in the second story that had improved from the previous year.

Every child has grown in every way — socially, cognitively and emotionally — even physically. The little desks and chairs are no longer adequate for some whose knees are rubbing against the undersides of their desks.

I had worried that we might grow tired of each other, but as the second year progressed, I found them even more fascinating. Their enthusiasm in their new curriculum never waned. As each unit of study was introduced, the children never failed to bring in relevant books and artifacts.

When Jessica told me that she felt nervous about third grade, I asked her what she felt most nervous about. Without a moment's hesitation she said, "Having a new teacher."

Each year, it's difficult to say goodbye to my class. This year will be the most difficult. As I put away the second grade materials and prepare to return to first grade, I find myself reflecting on how lucky I was to be able to hold on to my class for two years. Now, I'm able to say goodbye and let them go knowing that I have had some of my most rewarding teaching and learning experiences with these children.

Deborah Jacoby teaches first and second graders in Chicago, IL.

Mr. Burke calls for serious discussion and widespread piloting of multi-year teacher/student relationships.

Multi-Year Teacher/Student Relationships Are a Long-Overdue Arrangement

by Daniel L. Burke

Most parents do not send their child to a new pediatrician each year. Rather, they try to arrange for a single pediatrician to monitor their child's growth and development over time. Presumably, these parents conclude that one doctor's growing knowledge of their child makes the management of that child's health care more effective.

Similarly, research on school effectiveness has consistently suggested that long-term teacher/student relationships improve both student performance[1] and job satisfaction for teachers.[2] Yet, despite these findings, meaningful discussion of long-term teacher-student relationships is scarce in our nation's schools, and implementation is rare enough to be regarded as exceptional.

A close look at the literature makes the scarcity of discussion and the rarity of implementation of multi-year teacher/student relationships puzzling. For example, one group of teachers who taught the same students for three years told researcher Nancy Doda that the experience had been the "most satisfying" interval of their professional lives because it allowed them "to see students grow and change over time."[3]

Teachers in a different school using the same organizational plan affirmed these findings.[4] Approximately 70% of them reported that teaching the same students for three years allowed them to use more positive approaches to classroom management. Ninety-two percent of them said that they knew more about their students, and 69% described their students as more willing to participate voluntarily in class. Eighty-five percent of the teachers reported that their students were better able to see themselves as important members of a group, to feel pride in that group, and to feel pride in the school as a whole. Eighty-four percent of the teachers reported more positive relationships with parents, and 75% reported increased empathy with colleagues. The reactions of students in this study were favorable as well, and they grew more positive with each successive grade level. Parents also responded positively; indeed, when allowed to request teachers for their children, 99% of parents requested the same teacher to whom their child had been assigned during the previous year.

Meanwhile, some "comprehensive" schools in what was then West Germany kept teachers and students together for six years.[5] Ann Ratzki, headmistress of one of those schools, said that she has never found it necessary to switch a student from one teacher to another because of serious personality conflicts.[6]

Further, Ratzki noted:

We don't lose several weeks each September learning a new set of names, teaching the basic rules to a new set of students, and figuring out exactly what they learned the previous year; and we don't lose weeks at the end of the year packing students back up. Most important . . . teachers get to know how each student learns . . . The importance of this is incalculable.[7]

A 1990 article on students as citizens described multi-year teacher/student relationships as one means "to make sure that every child has the time to connect with the classroom, feel a part of all that goes on, and have the time it takes to succeed in school."[8]

The fact that model and pilot programs that seek to create multi-year teacher/student relationships are starting to show up in U.S. schools is encouraging. One of the more ambitious models can be found in Attleboro, Massachusetts, a K-12 district serving 6,000 students. When he started that pilot program three years ago, Superintendent Joseph Rappa asked "26 elementary and middle school teachers to stay with a group of students for two years in an experiment he hoped would improve learning."[9] According to Assistant Superintendent Theodore Thibodeau, by fall of 1994 the two-year teacher/student relationship model in Attleboro will have 100% staff participation in grades 1 through 8, and district officials will begin phasing in a similar arrangement in grades 9 through 12.

Mary Blythe, a middle school teacher in the Attleboro system, typifies her colleagues' enthusiasm for this concept. "It's the most exciting thing I've done, and I'm 55 years old," she said. "Seeing the eagerness with which youngsters participate and are engaged in their learning is thrilling."[10]

Maryann Pour Previti, the principal of Worcester Central Catholic Elementary School in Worcester, Massachusetts, has a similar view of multi-year teacher/student relationships. Previti has three teachers who are spending two years with the same students, and she describes those teachers as "the happiest people in my building." She also reports that returning students "step back into the classrooms with ease" and says that the three teachers have established "excellent parent/teacher rapport." Indeed, Previti is so enthusiastic about multi-year teacher/student relationships that she plans to expand their use in her building *and* to make such relationships the focus of her doctoral dissertation.

District 34 in Antioch, Illinois, began piloting the two-year teacher/student relationship model in the fall of 1994, starting with five teacher volunteers in grades K-5. According to Donald Skidmore, who was superintendent at the time, "It just makes no sense for teachers and children to have to learn a brand-new set of expectations from one another every 10 months." And that is particularly true, he added, "When you consider how much quality learning time is lost at the start of each school year in the traditional single-year arrangement." In Skidmore's view, multi-year teacher/student relationships also offer tremendous potential for summertime learning, because teachers can assign reading lists and high-interest projects to students at the end of the school year and then review and reinforce their efforts when they return in the fall.

Orchard Lake Middle School in West Bloomfield, Minnesota, is currently using a three-year teacher/student relationship model. Principal Esther Peterson describes her school's initial program as a "school-within-a-school." Selected students entering grade 6 were placed with the same two core teachers for mathematics/science and language arts/social studies from grade 6 through grade 8. Peterson piloted the program in 1993 with 54 self-nominated students and two teacher volunteers. She expected the program to improve student attendance, increase student involvement in school activities, raise students' grade-point averages, and increase parents' interest in their children's education — and her expectations were realized. The program has since been expanded in response to student, parent, and staff interest.

Despite the examples cited here, multi-year teacher/student relationships are still uncommon in U.S. schools. But research findings and the enthusiasm of participants in multi-year relationships suggest that the arrangement merits serious discussion and widespread piloting. As is true of most innovations in the schools, however, educational leadership is the essential catalyst.

1. Paul S. George, *Long-Term Teacher-Student Relationships: A Middle School Case Study* (Columbus, Ohio: National Middle School Association, 1987), p. 3.
2. Paul S. George and Lynn L. Oldaker, *Evidence for the Middle School* (Columbus, Ohio: National Middle School Association, 1985), p. 11.
3. Ibid.
4. George, pp. 1-27.
5. "Creating a School Community: One Model of How It Can Be Done," *American Educator*, Spring 1988, pp. 10-17, 38-43.
6. Ibid, p. 14.
7. Ibid.
8. George H. Wood, "Teaching for Democracy," *Educational Leadership*, November 1990, p. 34.
9. Thomas Grillo, "Attleboro Keeps Teacher, Class Together," *Boston Globe*, 27 October 1992, p. 24.
10. Ibid.

Daniel L. Burke is a superintendent of Antioch (Ill.) School District 34.

Deciding to Loop

A decision to loop can be as simple as a principal saying to you, on the last day of school, "Mrs. Hartwell ran off to Bogata with the bus driver; can you move up a grade next fall? You can take your class with you!"

It can be that simple; but if you're the one initiating the concept in your school, a little planning is required, especially if you want to optimize the benefits of looping.

First you need to find another teacher, either in the grade above you or below you, who shares your enthusiasm for potential long-term relationships with his or her students, and who enjoys working with the students' parents on an in-depth basis.

You need to read the literature that exists on looping and long-term teacher-student relationships (see bibliography, page 141), then approach your principal with the concept. Once you get support from your principal, contact a school that has been looping for a few years (a number of schools are profiled in this book), and arrange for a visit. Be prepared to ask lots of questions:

- Did you enjoy having the same children for two or more years?
- How have the children benefited from two or three years with you?
- How have the parents responded?
- How has your relationship with the parents changed?
- Did you enjoy working with the same group of parents for two or more years?
- How much work did changing grade levels involve? Do you feel that it was a positive experience? Why?
- How did you adapt to dealing with children at different developmental stages? Did you enjoy it? (This is an important consideration. Second graders and third graders can express themselves very differently, depending on where they're at in terms of development. Some teachers may enjoy second graders immensely, but find teaching third grade a thoroughly harrowing experience.)
- What problems did you encounter? How did you solve them?
- What would you do differently if you could start all over again?
- Do you want to loop again?

Jan Jubert, a first-second grade looping teacher in Lac du Flambeau, Wisconsin, says,

> I wish I'd known skills, when I started out, on setting expectations and standards of behavior, little tricks of the trade to get the children learning more quickly and working well with each other, and becoming more self-directed.

Jubert has developed strategies for developing cooperative and caring behaviors and for spiraling learning using multiple intelligences and other instructional techniques, right from the beginning of the school year. These strategies give her first grade students a jump start on their education, which follows them through their two-year stay with her. (See "*A Good Beginning*," page 33.)

The Two-Teacher Partnership

When entering a looping relationship with another teacher, you need to work out an agreement which covers all possible events. What happens if you get to the end of the first year and one of you decides you don't want to loop — either the teacher due to move up doesn't want to teach that particular class of children for a second year, or the teacher at the higher grade level decides to stay at that grade level? What happens in the second year if the teacher who has looped from first to second grade, for instance, decides she wants to stay in second grade?

All eventualities should be explored and resolved before the fact; it would be wise to put the agreement in writing and bring the principal in on the decision.

Avoiding Dissension at the Outset

Whenever teachers are involved in any education change, the door is wide open for criticism. By being aware of issues that can arise among staff members, most problems can be averted.

- Be careful not to create an elitist program by placing all of the school's gifted students in the looping classroom.
- Nothing splits a staff more quickly than unequal class size. Make sure your looping classroom has the same class size as other classrooms at the same grade level. (At the same time, be protective of your own class in terms of size. You shouldn't be required to carry more than your share of students.)
- Place the same number of special-needs students in your multiyear program as any other classroom at the same grade level — not fewer, and definitely not more.
- When students transfer out of your classroom be sure to take your turn receiving new students.
- Giving your classroom a regal-sounding name, i.e., *The Wonder Years* or *The Platinum Program*, will almost always give fellow staff members the feeling that you think your program is somehow superior to theirs.
- Publicly comparing the benefits of being in your two-year program versus being placed in a 36-week classroom always divides the staff. Always represent your program as one of several fine options at your school.

Staff Development

While looping is about as inexpensive as an educational reform can be, it's wise to allocate some funding for staff development. Workshops on looping, child development and developmentally appropriate practices, authentic assessment, cooperative learning, theme-based instruction, multiple intelligences, and learning centers, as well as training in grade-specific curriculum requirements, will help a teacher make the most of her two or three years with her students.

Balancing Your Class Population

Mid-spring is when most schools put together their class rosters, and administrators considering beginning a looping program should start thinking about balancing next year's class population at this time.

Any classroom can benefit from a little foresight in terms of class composition; but when you're thinking of keeping the same group of children together over a two- or three-year period, creating a balanced class becomes even more important. Try to balance your class in terms of:

- gender
- ability levels
- racial and cultural background
- economic background
- linguistic background
- special needs

Providing a diverse, yet manageable class population will allow you to optimize the learning that takes place between students in any classroom, and that will only expand in a close-knit, caring, multiyear environment.

You also need to be careful not to overload your class with high-maintenance or special-needs kids. Because multiyear arrangements help the children who need help the most, there may be a tendency on the part of the administration to give the multiyear classrooms more than their share of these children.

As teachers, we are all going to have to accept the fact that we will be having lots of children coming to school with lots of problems, from now on. But these children need to be distributed evenly among all the classrooms in the schools, so that one or two classes aren't impacted more heavily than others, to the detriment of the students in those programs.

Before You Begin —

Familiarize yourself with the curriculum for all grade levels you foresee teaching, should you decide to loop. Your curriculum will probably be a hybrid of a single-grade, single-year curriculum and a mixed-age, continuous progress curriculum; you will want to meet the curriculum requirements of each grade level, but provide yourself with the flexibility to extend learning over the two-year period for students who may need a little extra time and work on some content areas.

Teacher Char Forsten says that one of the main benefits of looping is

> . . . to be able to teach to the students' strengths, while looping back
> to help their weaknesses. Sometimes you can only work so long on a
> topic before you realize that a certain child has had enough, and if you
> push it, you're going to lose him. With looping you have time to go on
> to other things, and then loop back and address the child's needs later.

You may already be using learning centers and theme-based instruction in your classroom; if not, now may be the time to explore some of these instructional strategies. They are well-suited to the kind of close-knit, cooperative environment natural to a multiyear classroom.

The Multiyear Assignment
Good for Kids, a Challenge for Teachers

It all started about six years ago when the school administration of Attleboro, Massachusetts, decided to tackle some of the problems Attleboro kids were facing. "We wanted to provide some stability in our students' lives. We have a lot of kids who move around a lot, and a lot of homes that aren't too stable," said Ted Thibodeau. The administration, led by Dr. Joseph Rappa, Attleboro's superintendent, decided to try two-year teaching assignments to provide some of the stability students needed. They began with small pilot programs at Coelho Middle School and Willet Elementary School, with a handful of teachers who had expressed an interest in multiyear teaching. Those teachers had very positive experiences, and "talked it up" with their colleagues; by the second year there were five or six teaching teams ready to try the concept.

By the third year, confronted with a group of enthusiastic teachers and evidence of substantial benefit to the students, the administration was faced with a decision. "We had to decide whether we were just going to go with the people who wanted to do it, or say, 'This is good for kids, so we're going to do it for everybody,' " said Thibodeau. "Dr. Rappa decided that everyone was going to do it." Now all teachers in grades one through eight throughout the Attleboro school system take part in multiyear assignments.

Today, the multiyear assignment has been accepted and is supported by the vast majority of teachers, students and parents, although "it went over better at some levels than at others," said Thibodeau. The teachers in the early grades accepted it more readily; there was more resistance at the middle school level.

"Seventh and eighth grade was the real battleground," Thibodeau said. "There were teachers who had been teaching eighth-grade science for twenty, thirty years, and they said, 'Now I've got to go back to seventh grade, and I've got to teach math and science?' We provided summer workshops in those areas where people felt they needed them, both in team building and in unfamiliar content areas."

In a survey conducted in 1994 by the school district, 70 percent of the seventh- and eighth-grade parents, students and teachers said they liked the multiyear assignment. "Today, that would be even higher," said Thibodeau.

A Reborn Math Specialist

One teacher who is described by Ted Thibodeau as "reborn" because of the multiyear assignment is twenty-five year math specialist Dave Cox of Coelho Middle School. Cox now shares a two-year seventh- and eighth-grade teaching assignment with his team member, Pam Puccio; he teaches math and science, while she teaches communications and social sciences. Cox spoke, enthusiastically and at length, about the two-year assignment and two-person teaching teams (see *"The Benefits of Multiyear Teams – Self-Esteem and a Sense of Responsibility and Community,"* page 95).

Simple Concept, Complex Structure

The multiyear assignment is essentially a very simple concept; but in Attleboro it's part of a complex collection of instructional strategies and structures that include emphasis on critical thinking skills, cooperative learning, and teaming of students and teachers.

Two- and sometimes three-person teaching teams are at the heart of many of Attleboro's classrooms. Teachers are assigned to a team by district superintendent Rappa based on a number of criteria.

"We're usually trying to get a blend of someone who's strong in math/science and someone strong in the languages, or in some cases male/female, in other cases veteran and newcomer," Thibodeau said. "The superintendent has made a number of transfers to achieve a better balance in the three middle schools.

"It's not easy for the teachers."

Although the administration makes the final decision about teaming arrangements, it will consider teaming requests from teachers. "We don't let teachers just voluntarily pick their teams, but when we know there's a bond that exists, and we know it's a positive one for the kids, not just something of comfort for the adults, we go with that," Thibodeau said.

Multiyear Teaming Improves Teaching

Dr. Rappa considers teaming a powerful administrative tool for monitoring and improving the quality of teaching in Attleboro. Not only does teaming allow the administration to balance the instruction in a classroom in terms of the teachers' strengths, but it is a way to build the competency of teachers who may be new, or may be less than adequate in their performance.

"New teachers are paired with a more experienced teacher; we don't put two new teachers together on a team," reports Thibodeau. "If we have someone whose performance is marginal, we pair that person with one or two teachers who are excellent, so that the marginal teacher learns or is challenged by his or her partners. We've seen a lot of improvement."

Multiyear Quality Control

Some people have left the system because of the pressure involved in multiyear teaching. One veteran teacher resigned after having received a less than favorable response from her group of parents. "We've had about five people take career leaves," said Thibodeau.

"Dr. Rappa believes that the multiyear assignment is actually a good supervisory tool, because in the long run, the parents aren't going to settle for mediocrity with a two-year arrangement. In the past they might have said, 'Okay, for one year we'll put up with it.' And if it's only in one subject area, too, parents will say, 'Oh, all right, we'll put up with it.' But when it's concentrated like this, the principal has to be a better supervisor; and we have to be very careful about whom we give tenure or professional status to."

The teams are evaluated every year, and are reassigned as necessary at the end of the two-year assignment. "Right now, the fifth and seventh grade teachers are beginning to wonder what's going to happen next," Thibodeau said. "We may move a teacher because another school needs a strong math/science teacher, or to create a better blend in terms of

Attleboro Public School District

100 Rathbun Willard Drive
Attleboro, MA 02703

Phone: 508-222-0012
FAX: 508-222-5637

Open to Visitors: yes

Contact: Dr. Joseph Rappa,
Superintendent
Theodore Thibodeau,
Asst. Superintendent

teaching style. One very good team [see *Kindred Spirits*, page 91] may not be together forever, because they're both so very strong, we may have to pair each of them with someone who needs some assistance."

Generally after teachers make a change, they're happy. "They get a new lease on life." Sometimes, when the team hasn't exactly been a comfortable match, the team members welcome the administration's initiative in making changes. "It takes the onus off them," Thibodeau said. "They don't have to ask for a team divorce."

Thibodeau provided The Society for Developmental Education with an opportunity to visit several Attleboro schools and talk with principals, teachers and students about multiyear assignments. See *"Developing Good Relationships with Parents — They Know Where I'm Coming From,"* page 73; *"Flexibility is the Key — Multiyear Teaming,"* page 85; *"Kindred Spirits,"* page 91; *"The Benefits of Multiyear Teams — Self-Esteem and a Sense of Responsibility and Community,"* page 95; and *"Class Dynamics — A Powerful Factor in Multiyear Classes,"* page 101.

Some Parent Opposition . . .

Most parents who've expressed an opinion have embraced the multiyear concept as highly beneficial for their children. Few parents — less than one percent — request that their child be transferred out of a classroom after the first year of a two-year assignment — an option that's been in place from the beginning of the program.

"That's mostly because the kids are happy with the team they're with; it may also be partly that parents are reluctant to stand out and make that choice," Thibodeau said.

"When the multiyear assignment is successful, the parents usually credit its success to the teacher; when it doesn't work well, the multiyear assignment itself is blamed." This was the case at a recent forum, where a small but vocal group of seventh- and eighth-grade parents spoke out against the multiyear assignment.

A Complicated Issue

Thibodeau believes that the opposition is about more than the two-year structure. "We have full inclusion; we have two-person teams, which means we don't have a departmental approach; we're dealing with some serious behavioral problems — kids that other towns might send away to a residential facility are included in the public school systems in Attleboro. We're a very diverse community, too, and we have kids with limited English speaking ability, and in some schools a larger Hispanic and Cambodian population, and that's part of the opposition, too.

"What some parents are really looking for is a return to a departmental, subject-specific, high-content kind of program."

Social issues get mixed in too; many more people are attempting to get their children into honors programs at the high school, partly in an effort to get them out of inclusive classrooms and away from behavioral problems; and the high school teachers are complaining, saying they're not getting the same caliber of student they're accustomed to getting.

"It's all very complicated," said Thibodeau. "A lot of different issues get mixed in."

. . . But The Kids Like It

The day after some parents expressed opposition to the multiyear assignment at a public forum, a team of 55 to 60 eighth-grade students met with representatives from NELMS (the New England League of Middle Schools) to discuss the multiyear assignment. "The kids were there, sitting on the floor and talking, and practically everything that the parents had said the night before, the kids said the opposite," said Thibodeau. " 'We love teams; we get to know each other.' 'No, we aren't limited in the number of friends, because we see them elsewhere; and when we go to the high school we'll have stronger friends, from having known them for two years, and we'll make other friends; we're not worried about that.' One teacher from another system said, 'There must be something wrong with it; doesn't anyone have any complaints?' and one kid got up and said, 'Yeah, the teachers know us too well.' "

This group had some special-needs students in it who took part in the program put on for NELMS, and, as Thibodeau said, "You never ever would have known it; they fit right in."

ATTLEBORO PUBLIC SCHOOLS
Interview Rating Form

Candidate _____

Interview Date _____

Address _____

_____

Graduate of _____

1. Attitude about learners   1 2 3 4
Accepts individual differences, but holds high
expectations for every student. Avoids tracking,
grade retention or labeling of students.

2. Theory   1 2 3 4
Applies educational research to everyday practice.
Creates stimulating learning environment and motivates
students to achieve. Adapts to developmental stages.

3. Instruction   1 2 3 4
Has repertoire of instructional strategies including
active and participative learning experiences that develop
higher order skills for all students. Skilled in mastery
learning, cooperative learning and the use of technology.

4. Management   1 2 3 4
Able to organize a classroom, plan quality lessons,
provide student routines, develop cooperative discipline.

5. Subject Matter   1 2 3 4
Has in-depth subject matter knowledge and
is able to design interdisciplinary instruction.

6. Assessment   1 2 3 4
Able to monitor student progress by means of
performance assessment and criterion-referenced measures.

7. Communication/Cooperation   1 2 3 4
Communicates effectively, both orally and in
writing. Works well with others. Demonstrates team spirit.

8. Use of Resources   1 2 3 4
Involves parents, school, and community
resources in enriching the learning experience.

9. Personal Qualities   1 2 3 4
Has positive self-esteem, leadership skills,
good health, energy. Motivated self-starter.

10. Background   1 2 3 4
Has appropriate coursework, training, and/or
experience for this position. Has positive attitude
toward continued professional development.

Total _____

General Comments
_____
_____
_____
_____
_____
_____

Candidate's potential compared with teachers in Attleboro is in:

1. Lower 50%   2. Top 50%   3. Top 25%   4. Top 10%

Interviewer _____   Date _____

*This Interview Rating Form provided by the Attleboro, Massachusetts School District gives
an indication of the qualities it looks for in a teacher. All teachers in grades one through eight
take part in two-year teaching assignments; all may be expected to be involved in teaching
teams as required by the superintendent.*

ATTLEBORO PUBLIC SCHOOLS

Interview - Writing Sample

Candidate _____ Date _____

Please compose a letter to parents of your students to explain one of the following:

1. How you will individualize instruction
2. The homework policy
3. How you will group students
4. Cooperative learning
5. The reading program
6. The major objectives in your classroom

ATTLEBORO PUBLIC SCHOOLS

Interview - Writing Sample

Candidate _____ Date _____

Please compose a letter to parents of your students to explain one of the following:

1. How you will individualize instruction
2. General letter on ADD/ADHD
3. How you will group students
4. Social skills deficits as they appear in cooperative learning groups
5. General parent letter on death of child in your school
6. The major objectives in your social studies group
7. What happens in your counseling group

The Attleboro School District requires a writing sample of prospective teachers, both to gauge their writing skills and to get an indication of the sensitivity with which a teacher may approach important and sometimes difficult communications with parents.

A Good Beginning

Jan Jubert believes in giving her children a good beginning.

Jubert teaches first and second grades in a small rural school on a Chippewa Indian Reservation in northern Wisconsin, some 60 miles from Lake Superior. Some of the children come from families with single parents, many of whom are having problems maintaining a strong family unit while trying to earn a livable family wage and be responsible "heads of the household."

"I've talked with many teachers from all over the country, and they're all seeing the effects these situations and the related problems are having on the natural growth and development of children, and on their education," Jubert says. "It cuts across all geographical, racial, religious and income groups. It's everywhere."

Boosting Academics and Discipline

Jubert was the first teacher to try looping at her school. It was begun as an experiment six years ago to offer a more consistent and quality education and raise low academic achievement and self-esteem among students who were having a difficult time adjusting to school and learning in general, and who were exhibiting serious discipline and adjustment problems.

Some of Jubert's kids have come into her class at the beginning of first grade with some very negative and aggressive behaviors. But by the end of the first semester of the first year, discipline problems are almost nonexistent.

How Does She Do It?

"I start off at the very beginning teaching positive social behaviors, building self-esteem and developing cooperative learning skills, with an emphasis on good, positive interaction at all times," says Jubert. The children take part in a "community circle" at the beginning of each day that incorporates games and activities to foster these types of social development activities. "They develop a willingness to share, and to talk with sincerity and genuine feelings; they really begin to open up and interact with compassion, integrity and individual responsibility." After about six weeks of this, Jubert finds there is rarely a severe behavior problem or one that cannot be dealt with rationally, effectively and efficiently. Most of the problems that do happen from there on seem to occur outside the classroom setting, such as on the bus or playground.

Starting Off With Multiple Intelligences

Jubert also begins each year with a two-week unit on multiple intelligences. "The children learn that everyone has a lot of intelligence with shared worth and value; some children are 'word-smart' or 'art-smart' or 'music-smart.' They also learn that intelligence changes from day to day and that they can use their multiple intelligences to learn more easily, effectively and successfully.

"Instead of emphasizing the differences between children in a negative way, we build on each person's strengths; then the differences among us become beautiful and very valuable," Jubert said. "The children do goal-setting based on their individual strengths and intelligences; their self-esteem flourishes as their success builds success." The emphasis on cooperative learning behavior and multiple intelligences translates into a real sense of responsibility, independence and achievement among her young students.

Before looping was instituted a number of instructional strategies were tried with some success, but a roller-coaster effect developed, with peaks and valleys of individual and group learning and social behavior. With the addition of the looping structure, both behavior and social development with academic achievement seemed to stabilize and improve.

Everybody Belongs

Jubert's class has full inclusion of special-needs students, including severely ED, LD and at-risk students. These students do very well in her class.

"Some of these children have experienced only how to fail, but they soon learn to overcome that. They learn that there is no failure in my room. It's miraculous to see what a looping class structure does for those children once given the chance.

"I had one child who weighed 40 pounds and was on 80 milligrams of ritalin a day, which I had to administer three times during the school day. With a lot of one-on-one assistance and understanding, and with fostering the development of responsible and independent behavior, he was down to 10 milligrams of ritalin a day at the end of the second year. He then moved out of the district and was taken out of the special ed. classification and placed in the regular ed. program."

Asked if she'd ever had to transfer a child who didn't fit in or do well with the rest of her class, Jubert said, "I don't move children out of my class." Period.

Adapting the Curriculum

Jubert feels that the hardest part for her in becoming a looping teacher was learning to provide a scope and sequence to the curriculum, at the same time spiraling it and making it make meaningful connections for the children. Also difficult at first was developing effective and quick ways to get the children to work cooperatively and positively with each other while becoming self-directed and independent learners.

She found ways to make the curriculum fun and interesting and to pace it to the needs and learning levels of the children. She is turning her entire two-year science program into a "Miss Frizzle" format, making a giant magic school bus model that will hold all the science center activities, experiments and extended projects from the science lessons.

She also introduced keyboarding skills in the first grade and fosters a lot of interactive and creative reading and writing activities using the computer and word processing programs. "It's amazing the learning that takes place," Jubert says. "The children can't get enough."

Teacher Benefited

Jubert feels that looping has forced her to stay flexible. "You can't teach the same unit every year simply because you or the children like it," she said. She has found her teaching to be more relevant and more child-centered; a byproduct of this is that it has become easier for her to motivate children and help each one succeed.

Looping Expanded

Jubert is finishing her third cycle of looping; at present, all first/second grades and third/fourth grades loop in the K-8 school. There was some discussion earlier, with differing opinions, about the school beginning a K-1-2 loop.

The first group of children that were looped in the first and second grades didn't get the opportunity to stay together as a group in third and fourth grades, so some of the gains they made were lost. Also, Jubert states, "I was not as effective or successful as a looping teacher during the first cycle of the 1-2 looping as I've become now." Had she known some of the things when she started that she knows now, she feels the effects and successes would have been greatly changed during the first cycle as well as for each subsequent loop. With the extension of looping into grades three and four, Jubert is seeing some positive results of looping sustained as the students progress through those later grades.

The Parent Connection

Jubert enjoys the strong support of her children's parents, largely because she communicates with them so well and maintains an honest and trusting relationship with them about their children and their children's education. She has developed a parent handbook for their use (excerpted on page 37), and has planned and successfully implemented family meetings, activities, and get-togethers.

At one time when looping was being expanded at the school, there was some opposition to the idea; and a vocal and interested group of parents actually went to the school board and strongly supported the program based on the benefits the program had actually provided for them and their children.

Transitions — Both Into and Out of the Classroom

Jubert pays careful attention to her children as they enter and leave her classroom. For children coming to her from kindergarten, she runs a week-long transitional camp with games, reading and activities that help acclimate the students to her and her classroom. She also provides a day of observation and collaboration for the teacher who will be receiving her students into third grade, to help familiarize the teacher with the instructional strategies that she has used and are needed with the children, and to allow the new teacher to meet, bond and interact with the children in their own familiar, secure environment.

There is a difference of opinion about the effect a long-term teacher-student relationship has on young children. Some seem to feel that it creates a more difficult time for children when they have to separate from a teacher after a two-year relationship; Jubert believes that the single-year structure, especially for young children, puts children in tremendous turmoil; they are not allowed to feel safe, secure and successful before they are "flipped" into another strange and new situation.

"The two-year structure," she says, "gives children a sense of security in knowing what they can expect from a teacher, their peers and the learning environment; it establishes profound self-esteem and achievement, promotes risk-taking and discovery and provides the opportunity to establish skills needed to become life-long learners." If in going on to their next class, they can feel some continuity and the same sense of security and direction as from the learning environment they're leaving, then perhaps this is all that is needed to make the difference.

Lac du Flambeau Public School

2899 Highway 47
Lac du Flambeau, Wisconsin 54538

Phone: 715-588-3838
FAX: 715-588-3243

Looping grades: 1-2
                          3-4

Open to visitors: yes

Contact: Richard Vought,
                    Superintendent
                    Jan Jubert,
                    Looping Teacher

A Look into a Looping Classroom

In her years as a looping teacher, Jan Jubert has developed a very successful discipline program, many valuable instructional strategies, and a content-rich curriculum for her first/second grade multiyear class. She has generously contributed some of them to us.

She has written a comprehensive handbook for parents of children entering first grade, which explains her program to them in clear, concise terms. (They receive a revised version at the beginning of their children's second-grade year.) The handbook provides a very detailed look inside her classroom.

The handbook includes a comprehensive outline of her first and second grade curriculum. Of particular note:

- A "Tribes/Inclusion" section evidences Jubert's strong classroom emphasis on cooperation and community.
- The "Ginn Anthology Readings" section reveals that Jubert uses a basal series (from Ginn Canada, and considered to be a whole language series); but the "Poem or Story Appreciation" section shows that she doesn't limit herself to basals, but exposes her children to a wide range of other literature as well.
- Her "Geography/World Civilizations/American History" section shows that she gives her children a wide range of learning experiences about the Native American Nations, of which her children are a part, without neglecting the rich heritage of other cultures around the world and in this country. (Jubert has covered the Native American Nations, especially the Ojibwe and Woodland Tribes, for many years.)
- The math lessons are from the Saxon math program; the fine arts, history, geography, world and American civilizations lessons include topics taken from the basic areas suggested in the Core Knowledge Sequence.

Jubert has also created a summer transition program for kindergartners coming into her first grade, in the form of a week-long summer camp. An outline of the program is also included here.

Parent Handbook (excerpt)

by Jan Jubert

What Is Looping?

Looping is the opportunity for students and a teacher to stay together for two or more years and share in individual growth and development in all areas; such as cognitive, academic, emotional, psychological, social, etc.

Looping provides a learning environment that parallels a close-knit family; one that produces and thrives on maintaining successful individual and group learning, cooperation and collaboration, positive social skill development and interactivity, and individual and group responsibility and independence in learning, growing, and developing into life-long learners.

There are many benefits from a looping program, but one of the greatest is the additional learning time that occurs because significant time has been saved at the beginning of the second year of each subsequent loop. This is accomplished by not having to repeat routine procedures and practices, reestablish behavior standards and expectations, and develop individual and group responsibility, accountability and independence in the learning environment.

Moreover, there are many other great benefits to looping, such as these that provide a student with:

- a sense of stability
- an "extended" family
- reduced apprehension
- strong interpersonal relationships and the time to build and maintain them
- enthusiastic attitudes
- a sense of community
- trusting and honest relationships
- the development of life-skills
- a stronger sense of community among teachers, students and families
- strong bonding because of a high comfort level
- an individualized and customized instruction and curriculum because the teacher knows the students and the content
- a tailored curriculum to foster higher academic and social expectations
- improved learning and achievement
- greater confidence
- a secure and safe environment to become risk-takers, an absolute necessity for learning and discovering
- a curriculum that builds on previous experiences and prior knowledge because the teacher was a significant part of those previous experiences and prior knowledge learning and activities
- the development of higher order thinking skills
- a greater opportunity to compare and contrast learning and learned concepts
- the opportunity to practice and solidify reading and writing skills
- an interactive community of independent learners

- an increased academic performance
- greater anticipation
- increased self-esteem
- an environment that promotes and achieves good mental health

Within a looping environment, your child will be given a quality education within a strong literacy foundation and a core knowledge curriculum that has been tailored and implemented by authentic assessment.

I am sure that you will find that looping will help your child to grow and succeed and become a positive individual; one that is happy and enthusiastic about learning and acquiring knowledge, by himself and with his friends.

In conclusion, I would like to share my very personal feelings about my experience and thoughts on looping. In finishing my fourth complete loop, I will once again put away my second grade materials and reflect upon what "we" as a "family" have shared; the triumphs and failures, the laughter and tears, the sufferings and celebrations, the work and the play, and at last, the bonding of sincere, compassionate and caring people. I find myself thinking once more of how lucky I have been to hold one more class so closely for two years and know that I have seen each and every child achieve academic excellence and greatness in their successes. I know that we have become true friends in learning and in life because we each cherish a small place in our hearts for what we had together passing through learning within the same time and space. I thank the students as they leave, for helping me grow into a better teacher and person, a true professional educator; created for them, with them and by them, using looping as the "vehicle that drives it all home".

August 1996

Dear First Grade Parents:

Your child will be coming to first grade on August 28th, 1996. Please help your child have a good beginning by bringing him/her to Mrs. Jubert's Open House and Get-Acquainted Reception on August 21st, 1996 between 5:00 and 7:00 p.m. This will be a very informal get-together for you and all your family members to meet your child's teacher, see the classroom, receive a Parent Handbook for Starting the Loop in First Grade and to pick out something very special to help your child "connect" to this classroom, his new teacher and the first day of school.

During the summer, I have been very busy planning and making lots of new units, games and activities for our classroom so that learning will be exciting, fun and interesting. You too, can help prepare for the first day of school by purchasing a backpack or tote bag that your child will use daily for homework, finished papers, projects, library books, activities, art work and notes for home. In addition to the backpack, your child will not need to purchase any other materials at this time. I will notify you when you need to replace important school "tools" that have been lost, broken or worn out. It will also be necessary for you to mark your child's clothing and materials with a permanent marker so they'll be easily identified and located. If you don't have a permanent marker, then please write a note to me indicating your wishes and I'll be happy to put your child's name on any of his things. If you already have some school supplies purchased, such as pencils, crayons, etc., put them in a small box and label the box "Tools for Doing Homework Assignments" and put the box in a safe place for easy retrieval Monday through Thursday.

I will be consistently adhering to my First Grade Discipline Program which insures every student an atmosphere and environment that is conducive for quality teaching and learning, with the opportunity to develop and grow together as a productive "family". You will find a copy of this Discipline Program in the Parent Handbook for Looping in First and Second Grade, that will be available at my Open House and Getting-Acquainted Reception. I will greatly appreciate your cooperation and assistance with this discipline program since it has proven to be very successful.

There will be many opportunities to share and assist in the development of your child's learning and self-esteem. I encourage you to work with your child daily on his/her homework assignments by prompting when necessary and always monitoring and reviewing your child's work when it's completed. Homework is a very important part of learning academic responsibility and practicing good study habits and study skills while developing better self-esteem through praise, accuracy and success. There will be many opportunities

Letter to new first-grade parents.

for parents and family members to share with the wonderful growth and development of their child. These positive opportunities will include monthly family learning and sharing sessions, classroom volunteer activities and situations, take-home projects, homework assignments and other materials to encourage positive learning interaction at home.

You will also be asked to assist the classroom in celebrating some of the holidays throughout the year, including your child's birthday. This help may take the form of sending in treats, coming in to help with games and party procedures or organizing the party specifics and assigning the workjobs to classroom parents and friends.

If you have any questions or concerns prior to the Open House on August 21st, please feel free to call me before or after school, between 5:30 a.m. and 5:00 p.m. at 588-3838, Ext. 112 or in the evening at my home, at ███████, after 6:00 p.m.

I am anxiously waiting to meet you, your child and his/her grandparents and family on August 21st at the Open House and Get-Acquainted Reception. Likewise, I am very happy to be your child's teacher and I know that together we will make this year a year of successful learning fun and academic achievement that will include many interesting and enjoyable experiences for you and your child.

So, until August 21st, I remain:

Sincerely in Education,

Mrs. Jan Jubert
First Grade Looping Teacher

General Class Information

1.   Your child will be provided with all of the necessary supplies and equipment to begin classroom work. You will be notified of any items that need replacement. He/she is required to have a bookbag or backpack on the first day of school and every day thereafter. Please send no trapper-keepers, toys, loose jewelry or un-necessary clothing to school unless you receive a note to do so.

2.   Label all backpacks, book bags, tennis shoes, jackets, etc. with a permanent marker with your child's name, teacher, grade and classroom.

3.   I will assist you and your child in becoming independently responsible for his/her own personal clothing and property. Students will need to be responsible for keeping their things with them until they get into their classroom, locker area, bus or home.

4.   Classes begin promptly at the second bell. Students who miss instruction with the class are definitely missing important interactive learning that can never be duplicated or replaced. Please see that unnecessary tardies and absences are kept to a minimum.

5.   Students tardy or absent must report to the office for a class admission slip. Please check with me for any information about the instruction, learning activity and/or work that may have been missed.

6.   The class schedule included in this handbook represents the schedule we will be following after the first few weeks of school and an adjustment has been made to the regular classroom routine, material management, learning formats and methods of instructional organization.

7.   We will be having several classroom parties and celebrations and ask that you participate in the organization, refreshments, activities and clean-up of one of these parties during the course of the year. You will be asked to select the one of your choice early in the fall.

8.   Students may be dropped off early, before school, or they may remain late after school with a prearranged consent and joint approval by the teacher and the parent. Specific activities for these times before and after school will be:

    tutoring
    make-up work due to excessive tardies and/or absences
    class workjobs and teacher assistant activities
    content center projects
    enrichment and/or art activities

First Grade Discipline Program

In order to provide your child and all of the other students in my classroom with the excellent learning climate and quality education they deserve, I will be utilizing the following discipline program. I have found this discipline plan to be highly successful and quick to produce positive results within a pleasant framework for all students and adults.

My Philosophy of Classroom Discipline

I believe that all students in my classroom can behave appropriately so as to learn to the best of their ability. I will not allow disruptive behavior to stop me from teaching and/or any other student from learning.

My Class Rules

1. To do the best I can in my work and my behavior.
2. To listen carefully and participate in all learning situations and activities.
3. To treat others with respect, compassion and integrity.
4. To complete homework accurately and on time.
5. To take care of our environment including any personal, classroom and school property.

If a student chooses not to follow a rule . . .

1. The first time he/she is reminded to correct the inappropriate behavior. Notation is made and the child's name is recorded.
2. The second time a repeat check is recorded by the child's name and he/she loses half of their recess time to discuss the problem and possible solutions with the teacher and/or his/her peers.
3. The third time is recorded with a repeat check and he/she loses all of his/her recess to discuss the inappropriate behavior and develop a plan of appropriate action to remedy the problem.
4. The fourth time the child receives a repeat check and a conference is held with the parents, the child and the teacher. The inappropriate behavior is discussed and a behavior contract is developed.
5. A <u>severe clause</u> is addressed here to deal with any severely inappropriate behavior that would be harmful to the safety and well-being of the child or other students. In such a case, the child must immediately be removed from his/her present environment for his/her own safety or well-being or for that of others. The student will be taken to the Conflict Resolution Room and a resolution conference will be held with the parents and the teacher and principal will be notified of the behavior and informed of any follow-up procedures or behavior contract to be implemented.

Rewards for Following the Rules and Using Appropriate Behavior

1. Behavior is quickly shaped by providing individual and group rewards to those students who choose to follow the classroom rules and use appropriate behaviors. Some individual rewards may include, but are not to be limited to:

   classroom funny money called "big bucks"
   verbal praise and recognition
   notes and/or phone calls home
   extra center or computer time
   special stickers or stamps
   special teacher-related privileges

   Big bucks will be given for the following positive behaviors:

   neat and accurate work
   completed and returned homework
   appropriate class and social behavior
   completed daily assignments
   listening and following directions when given
   participating and contributing during instruction
   respecting others and the property of others
   participating in classroom workjobs

2. Group rewards will be provided to encourage the entire class to behave properly and cooperatively as a group. I will provide one of the following group rewards to the class when they have earned thirty-five tokens for observing the rules, behaving appropriately and working together:

> have an opportunity to buy from the class store
> have a class party (popcorn, popsicle, pizza or ice cream)
> have an extra recess or additional recess time
> have a video
> have a free center period
> have a treat
> do a special project or art activity
> any other student-generated suggestion

The following group behaviors will earn a class token:

> The total class exhibits good behavior at any one time.
> The total class returns finished homework on time.
> No playground white slips are given to any student.
> A compliment is given to the class by an adult.
> The total class responds and participates during instruction.
> The total class is quietly engaged in working and/or reading activity.
> The total class is productively involved in small group activities/
>   learning centers.
> The total class completes work for the day.
> The total class demonstrates good cafeteria behavior.
> The total class participates in doing their daily workjobs.
> The total class is present for instruction.

It is in your child's best interest that we work together on developing positive self-discipline and good learning behaviors. I will be in close contact with you regarding the progress your child, and his/her class are making within this discipline program. If you have any questions concerning this program, please feel free to contact me at any time.

I thank you for your support in helping me to provide the very best opportunity I can for your child to experience a quality education and successful academic achievement in a positive, safe, comfortable and enjoyable learning environment.

Please read the First Grade Discipline Program again and then sign and return this page to your child's teacher.

I have read and I understand this First Grade discipline program. I have explained and discussed it with my child. I will cooperate in helping to establish and maintain an excellent learning environment for my child and his or her classmates by supporting this discipline plan. I understand that I will be kept informed about the progress being made by my child and his/her class.

I want to inform you about the following problems or concerns and also make these suggestions and comments.

Signed ....

Dated ....

Child's Name ....

Responsibility Charts as Developed by First Grade Students

First Grade Students List Their Perceptions of Parent Responsibilities:

> Get us to school on time.
> Keep us well rested and clean.
> Give us good meals every day.
> Make sure our homework is completed and returned.
> Provide us with the necessary school supplies.
> Keep our house and clothes clean.
> Provide us with a home and nice things.
> Teach us to be safe.
> Love us and spend time with us.
> Teach us to mind, behave, be polite and kind.
> Give us chores.
> Limit the amount of TV we watch.
> Teach us about God.

First Grade Students List Their Perceptions of Teacher Responsibilities:

> Be on time!
> Have work ready.
> Give good directions.
> Help us learn.
> Keep work interesting and enjoyable.
> Like children.
> Be enthusiastic and interesting.
> Correct our work.
> Be honest and fair.
> Like us and be nice to us.
> Keep good discipline.
> Enjoy teaching us as much as you can.
> Teach us to be good readers.
> Give reports to our parents.
> Look nice.
> Help children be organized and smart.

First Grade Students List Their Perceptions of Student Responsibilities:

> Be on time!
> Listen, follow directions and learn.
> Work hard and do your best!
> Hand in your work on time.
> Do not disturb or bother others.
> Have supplies organized and ready.
> Cooperate! Be polite and kind!
> Be honest with yourself and others.
> Keep desk and classroom clean.
> Respect others and the property of others.
> Obey the school rules.
> Keep hands, feet and objects to yourself.

First Grade Homework Policy

In order to make the best of the learning opportunities provided in the curriculum, students in this looping environment will need to work, study and apply themselves not only in school but at home as well. Homework will be assigned with the amount and frequency being determined by the needs of the students and the class. Homework is given to accomplish one or more of the following purposes:

1. Homework is given when specific abilities or skills are to be reviewed and practiced, especially in the areas of reading and math.
2. Homework is given as a means to extend, enrich and/or develop understandings or concepts beyond the regular curriculum.
3. Homework is given when the standards of achievement or mastery require more time than available within the school day.
4. Homework is given when excessive absences necessitate make-up work to be done at home.

Math and reading activities will be sent home daily, Monday through Thursday. Homework will not require a lot of time. All assigned homework should be completed within a maximum of fifteen to twenty minutes. Reading papers and/or books should be read to an adult several times and the adult should praise the child and ask for predictions before and during the readings. Adults should give the child time to use strategies they've learned on the "difficult" parts, ask him/her to think what might come next, or to identify sounds that they know in the unknown word. Later on, the student may state the main idea of the page or story, name the characters and give the setting. Then the adult should fill in the homework reading form with the necessary information, sign or initial and see that the child returns it the next day. Students should be encouraged each night to reread some previous stories and/or books from their newly created home library bookshelf.

Math homework will consist of completing Side B on their math sheet for the day. All of the concepts have been taught and/or reviewed during the day's lesson. Early in the year, an adult will have to read the directions to a first grade student so he'll know what to do. Later on the child will be able to read the directions by himself and do the problems with limited assistance. However, an adult will be expected to look over the child's work and help him to correct any misconceptions he may have had and give him praise for what he has completed and for the quality and accuracy he has shown.

All homework must be returned to school on the following morning. Parents are asked to initial the date box on the calendar found in their child's homework folder to indicate that they have supervised and reviewed their child's finished homework for the day.

There may also be another type of homework given, that of being an optional activity for over a longer period of time. Such homework may be used for extended learning and may take the form of games, models, art creations, nature activities, collections, etc. This type of homework would not be required and would be provided for children exhibiting gifted and talented tendencies.

Homework at every level will not only make the transition between grades and teachers smoother and less traumatic, but it will also provide for parents to monitor their child's work and progress on a daily basis and to help their child develop good study habits and the initiative to become an independent and life-long learner.

The First Grade Reading Club

We are once again beginning the First Grade Reading 100 Club. This is a library reading program that is done as homework either before or after the math homework. The books should be very easy for the child to read as they have been selected at the child's independent reading level. I suggest that you listen to the story several times as the child will want to read it to you more than once. Also encourage him to reread some of the books that he has read to you before. The children are usually very proud of their beginning skills in reading and they want to share with you their new-found interest and success.

After your child has finished reading, please enter the date, name of the book and your initials on the reading form in your child's homework folder. Your child may enter a new book on each line of this reading record form. When your child has read 100 books, he will become a permanent member of the Reading 100 Club. Later on you may list the type of genre being read along with other reading information. Please find samples of the reading record pages to be found in your child's homework folder on the following pages.

Thank you for your interest and cooperation in your child's literacy development. Together, I hope that we can provide the best literacy foundation possible and a life-long love and enjoyment for reading.

A First Grade Homework Reading Record				
Date	Title	Author	Pages	Genre

Child's Name _____

Student Contract of Responsibilities For A Looping First Grade

As a first grade looping student, I will:

1. Attend school every day I can.
2. Complete all classroom work on time.
3. Do neat and accurate work.
4. Use my time wisely.
5. Be prepared to work and learn every day.
6. Respect all people and property.
7. Be responsible for what I do and say.
8. Use appropriate behavior at all times.

Student's Signature _____

Parent's Signature _____

Teacher's Signature _____

Date _____

Child's Name _____

Teacher Contract of Responsibilities For A Looping First Grade

_____, your child's first grade teacher will:

1. Be responsible for being prepared and organized for instruction in each subject every day.
2. Be responsible for making sure that your child feels successful and safe.
3. Be responsible for being tuned-in to the needs and feelings of your child.
4. Be responsible for working together to achieve positive, educational outcomes and academic success and achievement for your child.
5. Be responsible for recording, monitoring and keeping you informed of your child's progress.
6. Be responsible for motivating and enthusiastic teaching, while positively interacting with your child.
7. Be responsible for using good judgment in making decisions affecting all teaching, learning and social activities.
8. Be responsible for nurturing your child's self-esteem.
9. Be responsible for making you feel welcome and helping you become an important part of the school and your child's classroom.

Teacher's Signature _____

Date _____

Parent's Name _____

Parent Contract of Responsibilities For A Looping First Grade

As a parent of_____, I will:

1. Be responsible for my child being in school every day possible and arriving at school on time.
2. Be responsible for reviewing and signing my child's completed homework.
3. Be responsible for reading with and listening to my child read stories including those sent home as homework.
4. Be responsible for becoming involved in my child's classroom learning and school activities.
5. Be responsible for sending a note to school whenever my child has been absent or tardy.
6. Be responsible for monitoring the amount and quality of television my child watches.
7. Be responsible for providing my child with the appropriate food, rest and clothing.
8. Be responsible for contacting the school with any and all questions, concerns and suggestions concerning the education of my child.

Parent's Signature _____

Date _____

1996 – 1997 First Grade Looping Schedule

7:45 - 8:00	8:00 - 8:30	8:30 - 9:11	9:11 - 9:15	9:15 - 10:00	10:00 - 10:40	10:40 - 10:55	10:55 - 11:25
Social Skill Development	Math Meeting English	Music	Bathroom Break	Reading	Math	Writer's Workshop	Primary Computer Lab
Social Skill Development	Math Meeting English	P.E.	Bathroom Break	Reading	Math	Writer's Workshop	Primary Computer Lab
Social Skill Development	Math Meeting English	Math	Bathroom Break	Reading	Computers Chapter I	Writer's Workshop	Primary Computer Lab
Social Skill Development	Math Meeting English	P.E.	Bathroom Break	Reading	Math	Writer's Workshop	Primary Computer Lab
Social Skill Development	Math Meeting English	P.E.	Bathroom Break	Reading	Math	Writer's Workshop	Primary Computer Lab

11:25 - 11:55	12:00 - 12:10	12:10 - 12:40	12:43 - 1:11	1:15 - 1:45	1:45 - 1:47	1:47 - 2:08	2:08 - 2:40	2:40 - 2:52
LUNCH	AM Journal	RECESS	Social Studies	Science	Bathroom Break	Ojibwe Language	Centers	PM Journal Clean-up Workjobs
LUNCH	AM Journal	RECESS	Social Studies	Science	Bathroom Break	Ojibwe Language	Centers	PM Journal Clean-up Workjobs
LUNCH	AM Journal	RECESS	Social Studies	Science	Bathroom Break	Library	Centers	PM Journal Clean-up Workjobs
LUNCH	AM Journal	RECESS	Social Studies	Science	Bathroom Break	Ojibwe Language	Centers	PM Journal Clean-up Workjobs
LUNCH	AM Journal	RECESS	Social Studies	Science	Bathroom Break	Art	Centers	PM Journal Clean-up Workjobs

Definition of Learning Centers

We will be using learning centers throughout our looping program to enhance concept extensions and achievement, develop a spiraled curriculum and incorporate better learning through the seven multiple intelligences.

These centers will concentrate around various themes, curriculum concepts or daily content areas and lessons. The activities in each center will encourage further individual growth and development including cooperative and social behaviors. Interaction with peers, other adults and the teacher at these centers promotes cooperation, the development of life skills and positive learning experiences for each and every child.

Following are a list of centers that will be available in this first year of the looping sequence:

Reading Center
The Reading Center offers reading practice and experiences, listening cassettes and books, recording the reading of stories and poems, making puppets and acting out a story, working with the alphabet, letters and sounds, playing reading games, doing reading computer programs and doing sentence puzzles.

Writing Center
The Writing Center has books to reproduce and innovate, pictures to put to text and text to pictures, pictionary and dictionary work to do, cards to write, webs and graphic organizers to do, letter writing activities, computer keyboarding, computer word processing and making journal entries.

Math Center
The Math Center has manipulatives to use, math games to play, number facts to do, computer programs to do and number books to make.

Science Center
The Science Center offers experiments, video tapes, science games, observing, discovering and reporting activities, science book readings, science book reproductions, the drawing of diagrams, the making of models, computer science programs, and the graphing of information.

Social Studies Center
The Social Studies Center will have self-esteem activities and projects, map work to do, crafts and flags to make from around the world, games to play, computer programs to do, books to make and models to create.

Fine Arts Center
This center will have painting, mural making, model building, sculpturing, drawing, creating dioramas and movies, dancing, singing and acting opportunities.

TIPS FOR WORKING WITH YOUR CHILD

· Set up an area for your child's books and homework materials.

· Make frequent trips to your child's classroom.

· Provide books for your child and take time to share and read the stories together.

· Establish a regular time for you and your child to read together and do his/her homework.

· Become involved in the monthly parent activities at school.

· Play with your child and help him feel confident in what he can do.

· Talk about reading, words and letters in the environment around you and wherever you may be with your child.

· Show your child, don't just tell him that learning and school are important. Turn off the TV and talk, read or play games together.

· Talk with your child about the new things he or she may be learning and/or doing in school like computers, new math, geography, etc.

· Do holiday preparations and/or projects with your child.

· Help your child begin a collection. (Postcards, stamps, rocks, stickers, pogs, shells, etc. may be one of interest.)

· Have your child cook with you, explain measurements, different foods, the directions one needs to follow and the ingredients that are needed. Enjoy the "special" things and little jobs that you can share.

· Talk about coins and their value and have your child practice counting pennies, dimes or nickels.

Language Learning Experiences

There will be many opportunities this year for your child to develop his/her language skills and begin to establish a foundation of literacy in listening, speaking, reading and writing.

Listening skills are an important part of our looping program. Children must learn to listen carefully in order to learn new facts and ideas and to understand how to put these ideas and concepts into productive outcomes. Listening is also very instrumental in hearing, understanding and following directions in all types of learning situations. The development of listening skills will be accomplished in large and small group settings and in individual center activities and learning lessons.

Reading will be done on the first day of school and will always be given top priority in the looping classroom. Research has proven that children learn to read by reading and so we will be doing a large amount and variety of reading throughout every day. The emphasis will be on reading for meaning, to understand the message in the author's text and to develop fluency and ease.

Writing will be a major part of the language arts and reading program because reading and writing go hand-in-hand. Just as reading is **getting** the meaning of words written by another, so then writing is the process of **giving** meaning to someone else by putting thoughts into written words. Daily writing is greatly emphasized throughout the looping sequence beginning with a discussion or brainstorming of ideas, followed by the development of a plan, web or outline, then the creation of a rough draft by using the graphic organizer completed earlier, then there's a peer editing process, a story revision or reworking and finally there's the writing of a final draft and/or the publishing of the story. When children begin to write, they will be encouraged to use invented spelling, or to write all the letters that they hear and not to worry about the "correct" spelling. This enables the child to write his/her ideas freely and to gain confidence and pride in his/her work.

Later as they develop their writing skills, we will address the use of correct spelling, punctuation and grammar that is needed to promote understanding and give meaning when they share or publish their stories. Writing is also an important activity to be done as often as possible in school as well as at home.

The child's spelling skills will improve as he or she reads and writes. Children must be exposed to words in reading and writing a long time before they become competent spellers on a regular basis.

Speaking is a great skill to develop and one that is highly advantageous to possess. Therefore, we will have many opportunities to discuss and verbally share ideas and opinions and to ask questions and express one's feelings and observations. Students will learn to use the appropriate speaking skills when addressing a partner, a small group or a large group and/or communicating with adults, peers, younger or older children. We will also develop the corresponding social skills necessary to use when speaking and students will learn to use different speaking attributes depending on the type of presentation that will be made.

Music also helps to develop language and language patterns. Children will read and learn new words as they learn and sing new songs. They will experiment with sound, rhythm, movement and rhyme. They will enjoy developing their language through singing and remembering "connected" words and tunes.

Multiple Intelligences in a Looping Program

All children possess many different types of intelligences. There are seven intelligences that we know about, seven different ways of being smart. Students will learn to identify and relate to these seven different intelligences by engaging in learning activities that promote and develop each of these intelligences. In a looping sequence, students will learn to use their stronger intelligences while developing their weaker ones so that optimum learning will be occurring at all times. Students will learn to transfer the use of their multiple intelligences into all types of living and learning situations.

Students will improve their self-esteem through using their multiple intelligences and being able to recognize and identify the characteristics of each and how they are used. They will accept others as valuable participants and contributors in the academic and social environment because of the strengths and the variety of multiple intelligences that each child brings to the process of learning, growing and developing together.

In the looping sequence it will be necessary for all students to be able to identify and utilize their strengths in order to learn in the best possible way with the greatest pleasure, enjoyment and collaboration. They must also be aware of other intelligences that they possess and learn how to develop them in order to be more successful and productive. It is also necessary for all students/people to recognize the multiple intelligences strengths and needs in others so as to be able to accept others as valuable "equals" in the learning process and in our global community.

THE SEVEN MULTIPLE INTELLIGENCES INCLUDE THE:

	or in kids's talk	
Verbal/Linguistic		Word Smart
Logical/Mathematical	or	Number Smart
Visual/Spatial	or	Art Smart
Body/Kinesthetic	or	Body Smart
Musical/Rhythmic	or	Music Smart
Interpersonal	or	People Smart
Intrapersonal	or	Self Smart

Jan Jubert's First- and Second-Grade Curriculum
First Grade

August/September

Tribes / Inclusion

Community Circle
Two on a Crayon
What Feelings Do You Have
Abstract Painting Feelings
Pantomime

Math

Saxon Math Lessons 1-20
Calendar work and math meeting
Identifying sets and numbers for 0-18
Identify shapes and characteristics for circle,
  square and triangle
Ordering sets smallest to largest
Identify fewest, most, morning, afternoon,
  first, last, between, first, second, third,
  inside, outside
Acting out some, some more and some,
  some went away stories
Sorting by one attribute
Counting pennies
Season: fall
Divide solid in half
Graph a picture on a pictograph
Picturing and combining sets

Language Arts Skills

Listen attentively during formal and informal
  situations with peers and adults
Listen to and follow oral directions
Maintain subject line in conversation
Retell a story with complete beginning,
  middle and end
Role-play using dialogue in skit/play
Identify consonant sounds in initial, medial
  and final positions: c, d, g, m, l, h, t
Blend sound/symbols to decode
Acquires 10 basic sight words
Identify and utilize short vowel sounds:
  a, e, i, o, u
Identify plurals and their meaning

Ginn Anthology Readings
Level 1

Fishing
I Like the Rain
A House for a Mouse
Supper for a Troll
Horrible Thing With Hairy Feet
Stacks of Caps
The Gumby Shop

October

Tribes / Inclusion

Fuzzyland Map
Warm Fuzzies
Spider Web
Five Tribes
My Favorite People
People Puzzles

Math

Saxon Math Lessons 21-36
Calendar work and math meeting
Writing numbers 19-33
Writing addition sentences
Ordinal numbers to the 6th
Addition facts - Doubles to 20
Identify rectangle and its attributes
Identify attributes of pattern blocks
Identify heavier and lighter using a balance
Order numbers to 20
Add one to a number
Write subtraction sentences
Count backward from 10 to 0
Identify morning, afternoon and night
Measure length and width —
  nonstandard units

Language Arts Skills

Maintain previous reading, listening and
  speaking skills
Recognize, utilize and reproduce digraphs:
  ch, sh, wh, hard th, soft th
Recognize long vowel patterns: digraphs,
  dipthongs and the silent e
Acquire an additional 10 sight words
Maintain mastery of consonants and decoding
  skills for CVC word patterns
Review consonants: j, k, p, b, r, f, n
Retell a story with a beginning, middle and
  end, including characters and setting

Ginn Anthology Readings
Level 2

Hide-and-Seek
What Would You Like?
Know What I Can Do?
Pets are Fun
A Dragon for My Wagon
An Animal Alphabet
Can You Find the Wind?

November

Tribes / Inclusion

Wishful Thinking
Something Good
Singing the Blues
One Special Thing About Me

Math

Saxon Math Lessons 37-52
Calendar work and math meeting
Writing numbers 34-47
Adding one to a number
Sorting items — create a graph
Weigh objects — nonstandard units
Addition facts with zero
Identify identical designs
Covering designs differently
Counting by 10's to 100 and 2's to 20
Subtraction facts minus one
Counting pennies and dimes
Ordering containers by volume
Identify 1 cup measure
Identify/locate no.'s on 100 chart
Telling time to one hour
Identify even numbers to 20

Language Arts Skills

Maintain previously acquired listening,
  speaking and reading skills
Recognize, utilize and reproduce qu
Recognize, utilize and reproduce short
  and long vowel word patterns
Acquire an additional 10 sight words for
  a total of 30
Review silent e, CVCe pattern
Consonants in initial, medial and final
  positions: s, w, y, x, z
Identify main idea and topic

Ginn Anthology Readings
Level 3 — On With the Show!

What's the Funniest Thing
Knock Knock
Little Red Hen
Make a Puppet
What Does It Take to Make a Clown
Who Likes the Circus?
Where Are You Going?
Moonbeam on a Cat's Ear
Shadow Magic
Albert's Bed

August/September	October	November
Writing	**Writing**	**Writing**
Write about a topic and be able to read what was written Write a complete sentence Begin keyboarding skills	Use capitalization for a name, I and the beginning of a sentence Write two sentences relating to a topic Keyboarding skills continued	Use the punctuation of a period and a comma Write 2-4 related sentences Keyboarding skills continued
Poem or Story Appreciation	**Poem or Story Appreciation**	**Poem or Story Appreciation**
A Frog A Good Play Hope I Know All the Sounds the Animals Make The Owl and the Pussycat Rope Rhyme The Swing	How Anansi Got Stories from the Sky God It Could Always Be Worse Puss in the Boots The Knee High Man One Inch Boy — Japan Tom Thumb — England Thumbelina — Danish Little Finger on the Watermelon Patch — Vietnam	My Shadow Jack and the Beanstalk Sing a Song People Solomon Grundy Table Manners Thanksgiving Day Washington Rapunzel Rumpelstiltskin Why the Owl Had Big Eyes
Sayings	**Sayings**	**Sayings**
A.M. and P.M. An apple a day keeps the doctor away Do unto others as you would have them do unto you	If at first you don't succeed, try, try again Practice makes perfect	Let the cat out of the bag Sour grapes
Science	**Science**	**Science**

Seasons
Living things and their environments
  Forest habitat
  Water habitat
Oceans
	Living things and their environments
	  Meadow and prairie habitat
	  Underground habitat
	  Desert habitat
		Weather

Geography **World Civilizations** **American History**	**Geography** **World Civilizations** **American History**	**Geography** **World Civilizations** **American History**

Maps and globe, directions, oceans, continents, equator, poles, hemispheres, peninsula, bay, harbor, islands
 	
The Earth
  Its layers, identify and classify rocks, volcanoes, glaciers
	Land bridge, Ice Age/Stone Age
	Maya, Incas and Aztecs
	Early Explorations and Settlement
	  Columbus
	Conquistadors — Cortez, Pizarro
	English settlement
	Virginia, Jamestown, slavery
	Lost Colony, Sir Walter Raleigh and Virginia Dare
		Native Americans — All regions
		Past and Present: How they lived, what they wore, ate, their homes, beliefs, stories and current status
		Massachusetts Bay Colony
		Pilgrims at Plymouth Rock
		Thanksgiving

Music Expression	**Music Expression**	**Music Expression**
Steady beat, movement to music Beats have accents	Short-long sounds, fast-slow, pitch — high-low, loud-soft	Maintain previous skills
Songs	**Songs**	**Songs**
Skip to My Lou America	Frere Jacques Michael Row the Boat Ashore	Billy Boy Blow the Man Down
Art	**Art**	**Art**

Elements of art
  Color, line, shape, texture
Murals
O'Keeffe "Shell"
	Cave paintings
	Meret Oppenheim "Breakfast in Fur"
	Henri Matisse "The Swan"
		Portraits — Self-Portraits
		  Indian masks
		  Holbein "Edward VI as a Child"
		  Norman Rockwell "Triple Portraits"
		  Joan Miro "People and Dog in the Sun"

December	January	February
Tribes / Influence	**Tribes / Influence**	**Tribes / Influence**
Peer Response Huddle	Tribal Peer Coaching	Shaping Up With Blocks
Brainstorming	Thumbs Up, Thumbs Down	Resentment Appreciation
Chain Reaction	Find the Word	Tribe Portrait
Tower Building	Jigsaw	Paraphrasing
Confrontation	Third Party Mediation	What Will Happen Next

December

Math

Saxon Math Lessons 53-66
Calendar work and math meeting
Writing numbers 48-60
Counting by 2's and 10's
Following a recipe
Identify ½ and ¼
Identify even and odd numbers
Number clock face, time to one hour
Add two to an even number
Add two to an odd number
Sort, count, record pattern blocks used to
  cover a design
Compare and measure length
Subtracting zero
Subtracting a number from itself
Writing number words zero to ten
Identify pairs
Identify seasons fall, winter
Write money amounts with cent sign
Paying with dimes and pennies

Language Arts Skills

Maintain and develop all previous decoding,
  reading, speaking and listening skills.
Blends: bl, sl, pl, fl, cl, gl, dr, gr, br, cr, fr,
  tr, pr
Recognize, reproduce and utilize the
  suffixes: s, ed, ing, er, est and 's
Recognize, reproduce and utilize the
  prefixes: a, be, un and non
Acquire 10 additional sight words
Use cueing systems to assist in acquiring
  meaning
Will sequence four or five details from the
  story.

Ginn Anthology Readings
Level 3
Trade Books

Watch Out Freddy, Muffles and Percy
Here Come a Pig, a Frog and a Mole

Chapter 2 Level 3 • Home Sweet Home

In My House
In a Dark Wood
Toby in the Country, Toby in the City

January

Math

Saxon Math Lessons 67-80
Calendar work and math meeting
Maintain previously taught math skills
Writing numbers 61-72
Dividing a square in half
Subtracting half a number
Graphing pattern blocks used
Tallying — counting by fives
Use a ruler to draw a line segment
Sort common items
Add two-digit numbers using dimes and
  pennies with no regrouping
Addition facts — Doubles plus one

Language Arts Skills

Maintain and refine all previously taught
  decoding, word attack, reading, speaking
  and listening skills
Recognize, reproduce and utilize:
  contractions two-syllable compound words
Acquires an additional 10 sight words
Blends: sp, sw, sn, sk, sm, st
R-controlled vowels: ar, er, ir, ur, or
Abbreviations: Mrs. Mr. Ms. Miss Dr.
Identify character, setting and plot

Ginn Anthology Readings
Level 3
Science Trade Book

I Wonder . . . The Sky

Chapter 2 Level 3 • Home Sweet Home

House That Jack Built
Jack Builds a House
Three Little Pigs
Who Lives There?
A House is A House For Me
Animal Homes
Watch Out For Lions

February

Math

Saxon Math Lessons 81-97
Calendar work and math meeting
Maintain previous skills
Write numbers 73-88
Identify how many more
How many more on a graph
Make congruent shapes
Count large collections
Grouping by tens and ones
Trading pennies for dimes
Adding two-digit numbers with
  regrouping using pennies and dimes
Telling time to the half hour
Dividing a square into fourths
Coloring halves and fourths
Adding 10 to a number
Counting by 10's from a single digit
  number, adding 10 to a number
Ordering numbers to 50
Addition facts for sums of 10
Measuring to nearest inch

Language Arts Skills

Maintain and continue to refine all
  previously taught decoding, word attack,
  reading, speaking and listening skills
Recognize, reproduce and utilize graphemic
  bases: at, an, and, all, et, en, ill, ing, ot,
  and un
Acquires additional 10 sight words
Blends: squ, spl, scr, str, shr
Graphemic bases: ike, ame, ine
Vowel digraphs: ow, ou, aw, al

Ginn Anthology Readings
Level 4
Chapter 1 Out and About

Puppy and I
Beeny's Bike
Three Bears Walking
Come to the Meadow
Wake-Up Pond
Turtle Tale
On the Beach
We Were Tired of Living in a House

December

Writing

Identify and use correctly a period, question
   mark, exclamation point and a comma
Write four to eight related sentences
Write a five-part letter
Keyboarding skills continued

Poem or Story Appreciation

Wynken, Blynken and Nod
The Boy at the Dike
Sleeping Beauty
Pied Piper of Hamlin

Sayings

Land of Nod
The more the merrier

Science

Food Chains
Animal Classes
   Herbivores
   Carnivores
   Omnivores
Extinct Animals
Endangered Animals

Geography/World Civilizations
American History

Countries and Customs
World Religions
Modern Mexico

Music Expression

Patterns
Timbre-tone-color

Songs

Chiapaneas
La Cucaracha

Art

Diego Riviera "The History of Medicine
   in Mexico"
Goya "Manuel Osorio Manriquede Zunega"

January

Writing

Uses more traditional spelling
Knows and uses the writing process:
   Prewriting
   Rough draft
   Revising
   Editing
   Final copy / Publishing

Poem or Story Appreciation

Cinderella stories: Europe, Africa, China,
   Vietnam, Egypt, Korea
Native American
Pinocchio
Princess and the Pea

Sayings

There's no place like home

Science

Space
   History
   Accomplishments
   Time line
   Astronauts
   Rockets
Astronomy

Geography/World Civilizations
American History

Early Civilizations
   Africa-Beginning of humans
   Sahara Desert-Nile River
   Mesopotamia
   "Cradle of Civilization"
   Tigres and Euphretes
   Development of Writing
   Babylonia
   Code of Hammurabi

Music Expression

Music Appreciation

Orchestra
Classical music

Songs

For He's a Jolly Good Fellow

Art

Still Life
Cezanne "Still Life", "Apples and Oranges"
   "Flowers and Pears"

February

Writing

Writes simple answers to questions
Uses a simple outline to do research

Poem or Story Appreciation

The Pasture
The Purple Cow
Frog Prince
House at Pooh Corner

Sayings

Fish out of water

Science

Matter
   Atoms
   Solid, gas, liquid
   Changing states
   Property of matter

Geography/World Civilizations
American History

Colonies to Independence
   Thirteen colonies
   American Revolution
      Boston Tea Party
      Minutemen-Redcoats
      Paul Revere's Ride
      "Shot heard 'round the world"
   Declaration of Independence
   Thomas Jefferson, Benjamin Franklin
     George Washington
   Women of the Revolution

Music Expression

Music Appreciation

Classical composers
Music that can tell stories
Jazz

Songs

Yankee Doodle
When the Saints Go Marching In

Art

Jacob Lawrence "Parade"
Grant Wood "Stone City, Iowa"

March	April	May
Tribes / Community	**Tribes / Community**	**Tribes / Community**
Fork and Spoon	Rain	Wink
A Funeral for Put-Downs	Gallery Walks	Zoom, Zoom, Brake
Bubble Gum	Hagoo	Spider Web
Brainstorming	Hug Tag	Sharing From a Sack
Bumpety-Bump-Bump	Knots	Shuffle Your Buns
Clap Slap	Line Up	Skin the Snake
Creative Storytelling	People Patterns	Stand Up
	Spider Web	Zap

March

Math

Saxon Math Lessons 98-110
Maintain previous skills
Calendar work and math meeting
Writing numbers 89-99
Subtraction facts: minus two
Counting nickels and pennies
Identifying geometric solids
Dividing a set of objects
Identify a dozen and a half dozen
Subtracting a number from ten
Measuring using feet
Identify 1/2, 1/3 and 1/6
Addition facts: plus 9's
Identify quart, gallon and liter
Estimating and measuring capacity
  using cups

Language Arts Skills

Maintain and refine all previously taught
  skills in decoding, word attack, reading,
  listening and speaking.
Recognize, utilize and reproduce
  sound/symbol relationships for
  traditional spelling patterns
Digraphs: ph, ea, oa, ai, ee, ay, oe
Acquire an additional 10 sight words
Combines and utilizes reading skills to
  create related art and craft projects,
  science and math activities and engage
  in dramatic play

Ginn Anthology Readings
Level 4
Out and About

Crrrack!
The Chick and the Duckling
Down on Grandpa's Farm
Byron and His Balloon

Level 4
Once Upon a Time

I Like Stories that Begin "Once Upon a Time"
Three Billy Goats Gruff
Great Enormous Turnip
No Room

April

Math

Saxon Math Lessons 111-121
Maintain previous skills
Calendar work and math meeting
Writing numbers 100-109
Identifying one dollar
Identify fractional parts of a whole
Graphing tags on a bar graph
Writing observations about a graph
Counting nickels, dimes and pennies
Identify season: spring
Addition facts: last eight facts
Measuring using centimeters
Identifying geometric solids
Subtracting ten from a number
Adding three-digit numbers

Language Arts Skills

Maintain and refine all previously taught
  skills in decoding, word attack, reading,
  listening and speaking
Graphemic bases: ang, ong, ung, ink, ank,
  onk, unk, ight
Acquire an additional 10 sight words
Use some semantic, syntactic and
  graphophonetic cueing systems
Use and outline format to organize
  information

Ginn Anthology Readings
Level 4
Once Upon a Time

Tail Twists From Mother Goose
And the Rhymes Go On
Chicken Forgets
Deep in the Forest
The Magic Pot
If Wishes Were Horses

May

Math

Saxon Math Lessons 122-130
Maintain previous math skills
Calendar work and math meeting
Writing numbers 110-117
Subtraction facts-differences of 1
Drawing polygons
Identify and count quarters
Subtraction facts for doubles +1
Identify and count hundreds, tens and ones
Represent numbers to 500 using pictures
Subtraction facts — "leftovers"
Identifying the season — summer

Language Arts Skills

Maintain, refine previously taught skills in
  decoding, word attack, listening and speaking
Hard and soft c, g, and oo
Y and W as vowels
Begin independent reading of chapter books
  and author collections
Acquire an additional 10 sight words
Use more semantic, syntactic along with
  graphophonetic cueing systems

Ginn Anthology Readings
Level 4

Meet Beatrix Potter

Level 4
Trade Books

Frogs Can't Fly
Joey and the Detectives

Level 4
Science Trade Books

I Wonder . . . Wheels

March

Writing

Use keyboarding skills
Publish/share writing in a variety of ways:
  Word processor
  Make a book
  Act it out
  Read it to someone
  Put on a puppet show
  Tape-record it
  Make a display
  Illustrate or paint it

Poem or Story Appreciation

Hansel and Gretel
Medio Pollito
Aesop's Fables
  Boy Who Called Wolf
  Day in the Manger
  Wolf in Sheep's Clothing

Sayings

Wolf in sheep's clothing

Science

Human body
  Body systems
  Germs, diseases
  Illness prevention
Five Senses
Science Biography:
  Louis Pasteur
Science Biography:
  Edward Jenner

Geography
World Civilizations
American History

Ancient Egypt
  Nile River
  Floods and Farming
  Pharoahs
  Pyramids
  Mummies
  Sphinx
  Animal Gods
  Hieroglyphics

Music Expression

Music and movement
Ballet, tap, square dance

Music Appreciation
Songs

The Fox Went Out on a Chilly Night
There's a Hole in the Bucket

Art

Egyptian Art

April

Writing

Use correct keyboarding skills
Uses writing process
Publish / share writing in a variety of ways

Poem or Story Appreciation

Maid and the Milk Pail
Fox and the Grapes
Goose and the Golden Egg
Lon Po Po

Sayings

Hit the nail on the head

Science

Plants
  Plant growth
  Plant seeds
  Different plants and their uses
  Plant needs
Environmental changes
  Habitat destruction
Science Biography:
  Rachel Carson

Geography
World Civilizations
American History

Early Exploration of the West
  Daniel Boone
  Wilderness Road
  Louisiana Purchase
    Lewis and Clark
    Sacajawea

Music Expression

Music Appreciation
Songs

Down in the Valley
Dry Bones
Oh Susanna

Art

Van Gogh "Sunflowers No 2", "Irises"
Monet "Tulips in Holland"
Alma Thomas "Iris, Tulips, Jonquils and
  Crocuses"

May

Writing

Use correct keyboarding skills
Writes using the writing process
Majority of writing uses traditional spelling
Publish/share writing in a variety of ways

Poem or Story Appreciation

Tale of Peter Rabbit
Tales of Br'er Rabbit

Sayings

Never leave till tomorrow what you can do
  today

Science

Wheels and machines
  Steamboats
  Railroad
Electricity
Science Biography:
  Thomas Edison

Geography
World Civilizations
American History

Symbols and Figures of the USA
  Liberty Bell
  Current President
  American Flag
  Eagle
  Statue of Liberty
  Mount Rushmore

Music Expression

Music Appreciation
Songs

Take Me Out to the Ball Game
On Top of Old Smokey
She'll Be Comin' Round the Mountain

Art

Leonardo da Vinci's "Mona Lisa"
Whistler "Whistler's Mother"

Second Grade

August/September

Tribes / Inclusion

Community Circle
Ideal Classroom
Me Book
Teaching Listening
People Puzzles
Dream Quilt
Personal Journal

Math

Saxon Math 2 Lessons 1-20
Calendar work and math meeting
Read and identify no.'s to 100
Identify left and right
Graph data on a graph
Create and read bar graph
One more and one less of a no.
Telling time to the hour
Number a clock face
Determined lapsed time
Addition facts: Doubles to 20
               Plus 1
               Plus 0
Counting by 10's to 100
Writing to 100
Attributes of pattern blocks
Create and read a repeating pattern
Ordinal position 1st to 12th
Identify and act out addition stories
Compare numbers to 50
Identify days of week, weekend
Identify odd and even numbers
Identify common geometric shapes
Identify fractional parts of a whole

Language Arts Skills

Listen attentively during formal and informal
   situations with peers and adults
Listen to and follow oral directions
Maintain subject line in conversation
Retell a story with complete beginning,
   middle and end
Role-play using dialogue in skit/play
Review consonant sounds in initial, medial
   and final positions
Blend sound/symbols to decode
Acquires 10 additional sight words
Uses word form cues
Reviews compound words
Rhyming words-graphemic bases
Word endings and possessives; 's, d, ed,
   ing, t, er, est, y, ly
Suffix "ed" and related sounds of: (d) (t)
   and (ed)
Gives a short, simple oral presentation

October

Tribes / Inclusion

Fuzzyland Map
Warm Fuzzies
Galley Walks
Singing the Blues
My Name in Print
Snowball I-Messages
Boasters

Math

Saxon Math 2 Lessons 21-36
Calendar work and math meeting
Addition facts: Plus 2, Doubles plus 1 and
   Sums of 10
Adding ten to a multiple of 10
Identify and sort geometric shapes by
   common attributes
Draw and write number sentences for
   addition and subtraction stories
Divide a shape in half, shade half
Divide a square in half and fourths, two
   different ways
Telling time to half hour
Read a thermometer
Counting dimes and pennies
Create and read a bar graph
Identify missing addends
Identify differences in geometric shapes
Tallying and counting by 5's
Identify horizontal, vertical and oblique lines
Dividing a whole into halves, fourths and
   eighths
Identify missing numbers on a 100 chart
Identify pairs

Language Arts Skills

Maintain previous reading, listening and
   speaking skills
Recognize, utilize and reproduce short and
   long vowel sounds
Y and W as vowels
Recognize, utilize and reproduce all l and r
   consonant blends
Recognize long vowel patterns: digraphs,
   dipthongs and the silent e: ou, ow, er, ur, ir,
   or, ar, oi, oy, oo, aw, ew
Bases: ight, ind, eck, ick, ack, uck, ing, ike
Acquire an additional 10 sight words
Endings: vy, by, dy, ty, fy, ny, py, sy, ck, ge,
   dge
Retell a story with a beginning, middle and
   end, including characters and setting

November

Tribes / Inclusion

Silhouettes
Pantomime
Me Book
Joy
Creative Storytelling
Appreciating Others
Bumper Sticker

Math

Saxon Math 2 Lessons 37-52
Calendar work and math meeting
Measuring with 1" tiles
Identify tens and ones
Create and read a bar graph
Name fractional parts of a whole
Addition facts: Plus 9
Adding 10 to a two-digit number
Subtraction facts:
    Half a double
    A number from itself
    Minus 1
    Minus 0
Trading pennies for dimes
Weighing objects with nonstandard units
Measuring to the nearest inch
Counting nickels
Identifying similarities and differences in
   coins
Finding area using pattern blocks
Creating a bar graph
Create and read a Venn diagram
Identify line of symmetry
Create a symmetrical design

Language Arts Skills

Maintain previously acquired listening,
   speaking and reading skills
Recognize, utilize and reproduce short
   and long vowel word patterns
Acquire an additional 10 sight words
Soft c and g spelling patterns: followed
   by an i, e, or y
Three letter blends: str, sch, thr, spr,
   spl, chr
Endings: ble, fle, tle, dle, gle, kle, ple, zle
Follow a simple written direction
Write a simple direction
Identify main idea and topic
Identify topic

August/September

Ginn Anthology Readings
Level 5
Knock at My Door

A Difficult Day
The Father Who Walked on His Hands
Gloria, My Little Sister
See You Later, Alligator
Jillian Jiggs
First Day
Sara Brown Says Hello
Hey, Street
I Know a Lady
A Small Lot

Writing

Write about a topic and be able to read
    what was written
Writes 70 or more words per day
Writes for 15 minutes
Correct use of period, comma, exclamation
    point and question mark
Correct punctuation for beginning of
    sentence and first and last names
IBM Writing to Write Program
Keyboarding and word processing

Poem or Story Appreciation

Bed in Summer
Bee! I'm Expecting You
Caterpillars
Discovery
Seashell
Charlotte's Web
Emperor's New Clothes
Johnny Appleseed

Sayings

Back to the drawing board
Better late than never

Science

Life Cycles
    Birth, growth, reproduction and death
    Plants
    Animals
    Cold-blooded
    Warm-blooded
Cycle of Seasons
    Summer
    Fall
    Winter
    Spring

October

Ginn Anthology Readings
Level 5
Do You Hear What I Hear?

Sharon! Lois and Bram!
Lizard's Song
The Troll Music
What is Sound?
Sounds Great!
Mr. Whisper
The Surprise Party
Our Mole
Where Did You Get Your Moccasins?
Off to the Shop

Writing

Use capitalization for names, I, and the
    beginning of a sentence
Write several sentences relating to a topic
    and revise one of them
Uses the writing process
Revises more work for clearer meaning
Uses correct punctuation
Writes for 20 minutes at a time
IBM Writing to Write Program
Keyboarding and word processing

Poem or Story Appreciation

Hurt No Living Thing
Smart
Something Told the Wild Geese
Spider and the Fly
Fisherman and His Wife
Pecos Bill
El Pajaro Cu

Sayings

Cold feet
Don't cry over spilled milk

Science

Sounds
Weather
Meteorology
    Weather instruments
    Weather signs
    Weather reports
Magnetism
    Magnets
    Attributes of attraction
    Uses of magnets
    Compasses
    Electro-magnets

November

Ginn Anthology Readings
Level 5
Fur, Fin and Feather

Plodding Porcupine
Communication
Homer, the Hamster
Small Rabbit
Fox Eyes
Why Do Polar Bears Like the Arctic?
Flip, the Dolphin
Have You Seen Birds?
The Singing Bird
At the Water Hole
Frederick's Alligator

Level 5
Trade Book

The Green Street Three Play Tricks

Writing

Use the punctuation of a period, a comma,
    question mark and exclamation point
Uses correct capitalization
Writes 10 related sentences
Uses the writing process
Revises and edits with a partner
Creates an outline
Writes for an audience
IBM Writing to Write Program
Keyboarding and word processing

Poem or Story Appreciation

Buffalo Dusk
Ikomi Stories
Winiibozhoo Stories
Paul Bunyan
Casey Jones

Sayings

Don't judge a book by its cover
Easier said than done

Science

Animal Groups
    Classification
        Insects
        Birds
        Reptiles
        Amphibians
        Fish
        Mammals
    Characteristics, life cycles, helpful,
        harmful, solitary, social

August/September	October	November
Geography **World Civilizations** **American History**	**Geography** **World Civilizations** **American History**	**Geography** **World Civilizations** **American History**

August/September	October	November

Geography: Asia, North America, South America
 	
American Government
  Constitution
  James Madison
  War of 1812
  Old Ironsides
  British burn Capitol
  Star-Spangled Banner
Korea
Vietnam
Russia
	Native Americans — all regions
	  Past and Present: How they lived, what they wore, ate, their homes, beliefs, stories and current status
	Southwest
	Northeast
	Northwest
	Southeast
	Plains
	Basins
	Plateau
		Native Americans
		  Continued work on all regions
		Eastern Woodland
		  Sequoyah
		  Cherokee Alphabet
		Forced removal
		Trail of Tears
		Extermination of the buffalo

Music Expression

August/September	October	November
Beats, moving responsively, short and long sounds, fast, slow, pitch, loud, soft, melody	Like, unlike phrases, timbre, color, tone, verse, refrain, scale, notation	Names of lines and spaces Understand basic notion

Music Appreciation

August/September	October	November

Antonio Vivaldi "The Four Seasons"	J.S. Bach Prelude No. 1
	Mozart, Schubert, Chopin
	Mendelssohn, Saint-Saens
		Saint-Saens:
		  "Carnival of Animals"
		  "The Swan"
		  "Elephants"
		Rimsky-Korsakov:
		  "Flight of the Bumblebee"

Songs

August/September	October	November
America Old Dan Tucker Polly Wolly Doodle Star Spangled Banner	Cockles and Mussels Comin' Through the Rye The Erie Canal Loch Lomond	Buffalo Gals Clementine Get Along Little Dogies Good Bye Old Paint Red River Valley

Art

August/September	October	November

Elements of Art:
  Color
  Texture
  Line
  Shape
	Picasso
	  "A Mother Holding a Child"
	  "Four Studies of Her Right Hand"
	  "Mother and Child"
		Black Bear Bosin "Prairie Fire"
		Sculpture "Bird in Space"

December

Tribes / Influence

Interview Circle
Brainstorming
Thumbs Up Thumbs Down
Put Yourself on the Line
Animal Triads
Tribe Portrait
A Poem by Our Tribe
Files on the Ceiling

Math

Saxon Math 2 Lessons 53-66
Calendar work and math meeting
Subtract 10 from 2-digit number
Ordering 2-digit numbers
Draw lines using ruler
Make a number line
Measure to nearest foot
Measure geometric shapes on geoboard
Identify angles of a shape
Addition facts: last eight facts
Identify 1, ½ cup, 1 and ½ teaspoons
  and 1 tablespoon
Read a recipe
Measure ingredients for a recipe
Create congruent shapes
Make and read Venn diagrams
Identify am, pm, noon, midnight, dozen,
  half dozen
Add three or more single digit numbers
Write fractions using fraction notation
Adding two-digit numbers using dimes and
  pennies

Language Arts Skills

Maintain and further develop all previous
  decoding, reading, speaking and listening
  skills
Recognize, reproduce and utilize the prefixes:
  a, be, un and non
Use cuing systems to assist in acquiring
  meaning
Graphemic bases: ild, old, ind, ost, olt
Phonics rules: single vowel in word or
  syllable is short
Silent e at end of CVCe word makes the
  preceeding vowel long
Single vowel at end of word or syllable is
  long
Two vowels together the first is usually long
Acquire 10 addition sight words
Will sequence four or five details

January

Tribes / Influence

Chain Reaction
Tribe Mimes/Role Play
Peer Response Huddle
Jigsaw
Shaping Up With Blocks
Paraphrasing
I Used to Be; We Used to Be
Suggestion Circle

Math

Saxon Math 2 Lessons 67-80
Calendar work and math meeting
Add 2-digit numbers
Subtract 10 from a number
Read a thermometer F and C readings
Identify and create similar shapes and designs
Add 2-digit numbers trading pennies for
  dimes (regrouping)
Carrying with two-digit numbers
Subtraction facts: Minus 9
Measure and draw line segments to ½ inch
Use addition algorithm
Represent and write mixed numbers
Represent three-digit numbers pictorially
Identify and create over-lapping designs

Language Arts Skills

Maintain and refine all previously taught
  decoding, word attack, reading, speaking
  and listening skills
Recognize, reproduce and utilize:
  homonyms
  antonyms
  synonyms
Multiple meanings of words
Phonics rule: Vowels are influenced when
  followed by r, w and l
Identify character, setting and plot
Draw conclusion
Predict outcomes
Find proof
Identify story sequence
Acquire 10 additional sight words

February

Tribes / Influence

Confrontation
Family Camp Trek
Third Party Mediation
Tribal Peer Coaching
What Will Happen Next
Find the Word
What's in Your Wallet
Career Choices

Math

Saxon Math 2 Lessons 81-97
Calendar work and math meeting
Write a 3-digit number for a model
Identify and write addition and subtrac-
  tion fact families
Subtraction facts: Differences of 1, 2
  and 9
Telling and showing time to five minute
  intervals
Add three 2-digit numbers where sum is
  less than 100
Add three 2-digit numbers where sum is
  more pthan 100
Estimate and count large collections
Grouping by 10's and 100's
Subtraction facts: subtract a number
  from 10, doubles plus one facts
Create a bar graph — scale of 2
Write number sentences to show equal
  groups
Multiplying by 10
Covering designs with tangrams
Writing no.'s in expanded form
Writing money amounts with signs
Measuring feet and inches
Finding ½ of odd or even no. set

Language Arts Skills

Maintain and continue to refine all
  previously taught decoding, word attack,
  reading, speaking and listening skills
Identify root and base words with
  meanings
Word endings: en, ful, tion, ue, sion, ow
Ch as in school and ea as in head
Acquire an additional 10 sight words
Follow two or more written directions
Make inferences from text
Use cueing systems to decode and
  acquire meaning

December	January	February
Ginn Anthology Readings **Level 5** **Trade Book**	**Ginn Anthology Readings** **Level 6** **Stuff 'N' Nonsense**	**Ginn Anthology Readings** **Level 6** **What a Monster**

December

Ginn Anthology Readings
Level 5
Trade Book

The Green Street Three Stick Together
I Wonder . . . Inventions

Level 6
Stuff 'N' Nonsense

I Am Not Jenny
Making Spaces and Places
Good or Bad?
Amazing Magic Tricks
There's an Alligator Under My Bed

Writing

Identify and use correctly a period, question
  mark, exclamation point, comma and
  quotation marks
Writes for 25 minutes
Writes a five part letter
Writes a report from a research guide
IBM Writing to Write Program
Keyboarding and word processing

Poem or Story Appreciation

Night Before Christmas
Rudolph Is Tired of the City
A Christmas Carol

Sayings

Eaten out of house and home

Science

Tools and simple machines
  Wheel-axle
  Gears
  Screws
  Inclined plane
  Lever
  Pulley
  Wedge
Inventions

Science Biography:
  Elijah McCoy

January

Ginn Anthology Readings
Level 6
Stuff 'N' Nonsense

An Elephant in the House
Silly Snacks
Tear Water Tear
Not This Bear!
The Tale of Foolis Beaver
Too Much Noise

Level 6
What a Monster

The Dinosaur Dinner
What Happened to Patrick's Dinosaur

Writing

Continues to maintain previously acquired
  writing skills
Uses traditional spelling
Knows and uses the writing process:
  Prewriting
  Rough draft
  Revising
  Editing
  Final copy/publishing
IBM Writing to Write Program
Keyboarding and word processing

Poem or Story Appreciation

Peter Pan
Beauty and the Beast
There Was an Old Man With a Beard

Japan: Crane Wife
           Tongue-Cut Sparrow

Sayings

Get a taste of your own medicine
Get up on the wrong side of the bed

Science

Dinosaurs
  Eras and periods
  Specific characteristics
  Comparison of characteristics
  Difference among characteristics
  Create a dinosaur data base

February

Ginn Anthology Readings
Level 6
What a Monster

Let's Visit the Dinosaurs
Watch Your Step
The Dragon's Dinner
Pea Soup and Sea Serpents
Scary, Hairy Monsters
The Tale of Custard the Dragon
The Very Worst Monster

Writing

Continues to show mastery of
  taught writing skills
Writes answers to questions
Uses a simple outline to do research
Uses research and the writing
  process to publish a book
Writes letters, invitations and
  requests
Writes dialogue/conversation using
  quotation marks correctly

Poem or Story Appreciation

Harriet Tubman
Lincoln
John Henry
From Tiger to Anansi Talk — African

Sayings

In hot water
Keep your fingers crossed

Science

Dinosaurs
  Dinosaur data base
  Dinosaur research
  Book publications
  Related art projects

Science Biography:
  Daniel Hale Williams

December	January	February
Geography	**Geography**	**Geography**
World Civilizations	**World Civilizations**	**World Civilizations**
American History	**American History**	**American History**

December	January	February

Our Fifty States
Geographical features: horizon, coast, boundary, valley, desert, oasis, prairie, plateau
 	
Immigration, cities and citizenship
  Ellis Island
  Land of Opportunity
 	
Native American Nations
	Modern Japan
	  Geography
	  Flag
	  Cities, industry, business
	  Sayonara
	  Origami
	  Kimono
	  Shogatsu
	China
	  Huang He and Yangtze Rivers
	  Confucius
	  Great Wall of China
	  Qin Dynasty
	  Silk
	  Inventions
	    Paper
	    Seismograph
	  Chinese New Year
	Native American nations
		Civil War
		  Controversy
		  Harriet Tubman
		  North vs. South
		  Grant vs. Lee
		  President Lincoln
		  Emancipation Proclamation
		Civil Rights
		Westward Expansion
		  Pioneers
		  Wagon trains
		  New travel
		    Erie Canal
		    Railroads
		    Steamboat
		    Pony Express
		Native American Nations

Music Expression

Music Appreciation

December	January	February
Review families of instruments The String Family Percussion instruments Mendelssohn "Violin Concerto in E Minor" Ludwig Van Beethoven "Symphony No. 6" Aaron Copland "Hoe-Down"	African Drumming Latin-American Music Carlos Chavez "Toccata for 3rd Percussion Movement" Aaron Copland "Fanfare for the Common Man"	John Phillip Sousa: "Stars and Stripes Forever"

Songs

December	January	February
Home on the Range Sweet Betsy from Pike	Auld Lang Syne Shenandoah Sometimes I Feel Like a Motherless Child	Follow the Drinking Gourd John Henry I've Been Working on the Railroad Swing Low, Sweet Chariot We Shall Overcome When Johnny Comes Marching Home

Art

December	January	February

Thomas Cole "The Oxbow"
El Greco "View of Toledo"
Henri Rousseau "Virgin Forest"
Van Gogh "The Starry Night"
	Lines and shapes with movement
	
	Hokusai "The Great Wave at Kanagawa Nami-Ura"
	
	Ando Hiroshige "Rain at Shino"
	
	Sculpture:
	  Wu Wei "Flying Horse" — China
		Art in Architecture
		
		Columns and domes
		Symmetry
		  Parthenon
		  Great Stupa - India
		  Himeji Castle - Japan
		  Guggenheim Museum - New York City

March	April	May
Tribes / Community	**Tribes / Community**	**Tribes / Community**
A Funeral for Put-Downs Bubble Gum Brainstorming Bumpety-Bump-Bump	Gallery Walks Hagoo Creative Storytelling Hug Tag Fork and Spoon	Knots I Like My Neighbors Community Circle Metaphor That's Me That's Us Creative Storytelling
Math	**Math**	**Math**
Saxon Math 2 Lessons 98-110 Maintain previous skills Calendar work and math meeting Counting quarters Multiplying by 1 Multiplying by 100 Finding area using 1" tiles Subtraction facts: last sixteen Comparison symbols: <, >, = Geometric solids: cone, cube, sphere, cylinder, pyramid, rectangular solid Add 3-digit no.'s greater than 100 Measuring and drawing line segments using centimeters Multiplying by 5 Subtracting 2-digit numbers Covering same design in different ways using tangram pieces	Saxon Math 2 Lessons 111-121 Maintain previous skills Calendar work and math meeting Subtracting 2-digit numbers Measuring weight in pounds Finding perimeter Writing observations from a graph Identifying parallel lines Multiplying by 2 Acting out equal group stories Counting quarters, dimes, nickels and pennies Rounding off to the nearest ten Drawing pictures to show equal groups Choosing a survey question and choices Conducting a survey Representing data on a graph	Saxon Math 2 Lessons 122-132 Maintain previous math skills Calendar work and math meeting Making and labeling an array Identifying right angles Writing no. sentences for equal group stories Multiplying by 3 Identifying intersecting lines Identifying perpendicular lines Writing no. sentences for arrays Writing the date using digits Locating points on a coordinate graph Multiplying by four Creating two graphs using dominoes Doubling a number Dividing by two
Language Arts Skills	**Language Arts Skills**	**Language Arts Skills**
Maintain and refine all previously taught skills in decoding, word attack, reading, listening and speaking Acquires 10 additional sight words Uses cueing systems automatically for decoding and unlocking meaning Sound-symbols ew, ei as in vein, ea as in great and ch as in machine Combines and utilizes reading skills to create related art and craft projects, science and math activities and engage in dramatic play	Maintain and refine all previously taught skills in decoding, word attack, reading, listening and speaking Acquire an additional 10 sight words Use some semantic, syntactic and graphophonetic cueing systems Syllable patterns and rules for decoding Use an outline format to organize information Reads a variety of genres and contextual materials Reads chapter books and author collections	Maintain previously taught skills in decoding, word attack, listening and speaking Acquire an additional 10 sight words Use word analysis and contextual clues to decode unknown vocabulary to derive meaning Affixes and root words and meanings Reads independently by choice Uses different strategies to read different texts
Ginn Anthology Readings Level 6 Far Away and Long Ago	**Ginn Anthology Readings Level 6 Far Away and Long Ago**	**Ginn Anthology Readings Level 6 Trade Books**

Red Riding Hood
Teeny Tiny Woman
Thumbelina
Shoemaker and the Elves
The Gentle Giant
The Giant
	Tit for Tat
	The Gunniwolf
	How Trouble Made the Monkey Mad
	Me Eat Pepper
	Tell Me a Story
	
	**Level 6
	Science Trade Book**
	
	I Wonder . . . Plants
		The White Moose
		Simon and the Knockout Yawn
		
		Independent Readings
		  Various genres
		  Chapter books
		  Author collections

March	April	May
Writing	**Writing**	**Writing**

March

Writing

Use keyboarding skills
Publish/share writing in a variety of ways:
   Word processor
   Make a book
   Act it out
   Read it to someone
   Put on a puppet show
   Tape-record it
   Make a display
   Illustrate or paint it
Writes a story with a beginning, middle and end
Uses setting, characters, plot and dialogue
Uses adjectives and adverbs to enhance writing

Poem or Story Appreciation

Greek Mythology Stories
   Prometheus
   Pandora's Box
   Oedipus and the Sphinx
   Theseus and the Minotaur
   Daedelus and Icarus
   Arachne the Weaver
   Story of the Swift-Footed Atalanta
   Demeter and Persephone

Sayings

Practice what you preach
Two heads are better than one

Science

Astronomy
   Constellations
   Greek legends/myths

Science Biography:
   Galileo Galilei

Geography/World Civilizations/ American History

Ancient Greece
   Geography
   Mediterranean Sea
   Aegean Sea
   Crete and King Minos
   Sparta
   Persian Wars
   Athens — Democracy
   Olympic Games
   Gods and Goddesses
   Great Thinkers
   Socrates, Plato and Aristotle
   Alexander the Great
      Macedonia, Tutored, Gordian Knot, Bucephalus
Native American Nations

April

Writing

Use correct keyboarding skills
Use writing process
Publish/share writing in a variety of ways
Writes a position with supporting statements
Writes answers to essay questions

Poem or Story Appreciation

Hercules (Heracles) and the Labors of Hercules
The Story of the Trojan Horse
Odysseus and the Cyclops

Sayings

Turn over a new leaf

Science

Human body
   Body systems
   Cells, tissues, organs

Science Biography:
   Anton von Leeuwenhoek
   Florence Nightingale

Geography/World Civilizations/ American History

India
   Indus and Ganges Rivers
   Caste System
   Hinduism
   Buddhism
   Traditions
   Geography

Native American Nations

May

Writing

Use correct keyboarding skills
Writes using the writing process
Majority of writing uses traditional spelling
Publish/share writing in a variety of ways
Writes using adverbs and adjectives to enhance writing
Writes for a specific audience
Writes with a purpose in mind
Writes with color and interest

Poem or Story Appreciation

Blind Man and the Elephant (India)
Tiger, Brahman and the Jackal
Magic Paintbrush (China)

Sayings

Where there's a will, there's a way
You can't teach an old dog new tricks

Science

Physical Science
   Chemistry (what, who)
   Physics (what, who)
Energy, heat and light

Geography/World Civilizations/ American History

Business
Free Enterprise
Money Management

Careers
   Goals
   Expectations
   Requirements

Native American Nations

March	April	May
Music Expression	**Music Expression**	**Music Expression**
Music Appreciation	**Music Appreciation**	**Music Appreciation**
Bach Mozart	Schubert Chopin	Mendelssohn Saint-Saens
Songs	**Songs**	**Songs**
This Land is Your Land 'Tis a Gift to be Simple Wayfaring Stranger	Yellow Rose of Texas	You're in the Army Now Erie Canal
Art	**Art**	**Art**

Line in Architecture
   Parthenon
 	
Sculpture
   "The Discus Thrower"
   "Venus de Milo"
	Representationalism
	   Albrecht Durer "Young Hare"
	   John James Audubon "Birds"
	   Paul Klee "Cat and Bird"
	   Matisse "The Snail"
	   Pablo Picasso "Bull's Head"
		Abstract
		   Chagall's "I and the Village"
		   Miro's "People and Dog in the Sun"

Setting Up a Kindergarten Transition Program for a Looping Environment
Within a School Summer Camp Experience

by Jan Jubert

1. Set the calendar dates, the length of time and the starting and ending time for daily participation. A recommended session to begin with is for one week, preferably in the middle of the summer, with breakfast and lunch being served and the length of the day to be as close to a regular school day as feasible.

2. Design a family letter of notification and explanation.
   - Use a "catchy" title for the program
   - Briefly outline the program and the activities

3. Program Goals
   - To establish a "family" learning atmosphere and environment through social skill development and learning activities.
   - To provide for small cooperative group learning experiences through center choices:
      Art Center
      Science Center
      Math Center
      Social Studies Center
      Music Center
      Language Arts Center
      Physical Development Center
   - To provide for large group activities with an emphasis on direct instruction, including teacher modeling with student practice and interactive learning activities.
   - To use computers to facilitate prereaders skills and a foundation for literacy development.
   - To establish an awareness and appreciation for artists and composers.

Let's "Kick-Off" to First Grade

All kindergarteners are invited to participate in a celebration of activities as we "kick-off" to first grade together.

Meet your first grade teacher and have a week of fun from July 8th through July 12th beginning at 8:00 AM and ending at 3:00 PM with children returning home on the bus or being picked up promptly by a family member.

We will have a great time doing art projects, songs, puppets, listening to stories, playing games, making books, doing experiments, and discovering and learning all kinds of new and different things.

If you are interested in having your child attend this summer camp program please sign and return the form at the bottom of the page to Mrs. Jubert, the office staff, or a kindergarten teacher. Later we will notify you of the bus schedule and any other changes that may arise. If you should have any questions, please feel free to call Mrs. Jubert at the school at 588-3838 Ext. 112.

My child, _____ , will be attending the "Kick-Off" to First Grade Program during July 8th through July 12th. Please reserve a place for him or her in the program.

Signed _____ Dated _____

Telephone Number _____

☐ My child should ride the bus home at 3:00 PM

☐ My child will be picked up by a family member at 3:00 PM

Notice to parents

Daily Schedule for "Kick-Off" to First Grade Transition

8:00　Breakfast Program together in the cafeteria

8:30　Sharing, Talking, Planning
　　　　Cooperative and Social Skill Development

9:00　Direct Teaching and Interactive Learning
　　　　Activities and projects from the areas of language arts, music, art, science, social studies, math and physical development

10:00　Center Choices (Maximum of two daily)
　　　　Art Center
　　　　Music Center
　　　　Language Arts Center
　　　　Science Center
　　　　Math Center
　　　　Social Studies Center

11:00　Large Group Activity
　　　　Language Arts
　　　　Prereading and writing skills
　　　　Interactive reading and writing

12:00　Lunch Program together in the cafeteria

12:20　Outdoor Play, Games and Activities

12:50　Rest, Cool-Down and Music Appreciation
　　　　Composers

1:00　Center Choices (Maximum of two daily)
　　　　Art Center
　　　　Music Center
　　　　Language Arts Center
　　　　Science Center
　　　　Math Center
　　　　Social Studies Center

2:10　Closing Journal
　　　　Goal Setting and Goal Review
　　　　Center Choices for Tomorrow

2:30　Singing, treats made by the participants and clean-up duties

---

Center Descriptions

Art Center
　　Small artists in residence
　　Artist techniques, strokes, composition and color
　　Painting, sculpting, murals, models, drawing, creating, etc.

Music Center
　　Composers
　　Music selections
　　Dance, singing, movement, body interpretation
　　"Singing books" and listening cassettes

Language Arts Center
　　Nursery Rhymes
　　Phonemic Awareness
　　Story readings, tellings and retelling
　　Listening tapes
　　Book reproductions and innovations
　　Puppets, flannelboard characters and drama
　　Magnetic letters and manipulations

Science Center
　　Experimenting
　　Discovering
　　Observing
　　Reporting

Math Center
　　Manipulatives
　　Number awareness
　　Math games, gameboards, cards and concentration

Social Studies Center
　　Self-esteem activities and projects
　　All About Me and My Family

Physical Development
　　Large Group Games
　　Small Group Games
　　Free Play

Social Skill Development
　　Talking Circle
　　Talking Stick or Talking Feather
　　Social Skill Development Games
　　Social Skill Development Activities

The Parent Connection

Parental support is the key to success for all students, regardless of their program placement, but is especially important in a multiyear relationship. Parents need to be able to feel comfortable with you and trust you. The benefits of parent involvement, once that trust is established, quickly become evident. According to Jan and Dave Ulrey, educational consultants,

> The children of involved parents do better academically, get along better with their parents, do more things with their parents, and have a more positive attitude about school.

> The parents develop increased self-confidence and more positive attitudes about themselves, are more likely to enroll in a program to enhance personal development, have more positive feelings about school and school personnel, are willing to work for the school, and become better helpers for their children.

These benefits are compounded in a multiyear situation.

Initiating the Looping Program

Once you've educated yourself about the benefits of looping and have decided to try it, you need to educate the parents as well. Here are a few things you can do:

1. Write a letter to parents describing the benefits of looping, and informing them how you plan to proceed.
2. Schedule an informational meeting for the parents, and invite them to ask questions. Familiarize yourself with the common concerns voiced both by parents and teachers, and be prepared to talk intelligently about them and about the solutions/preventative measures you will have in place at the beginning of the program. (See "Look Before You Loop," page 105, for the most frequently-expressed worries about multiyear teacher/student relationships.
3. If your school's structure permits, provide parents with the option of placing their child in either a looping program or a single-grade, single-year program. You may want to send out permission slips for parents to sign which request them to state a preference for their child's placement.
4. Again, if your school's structure permits, provide parents with the ability to opt out of the multiyear classroom if they are dissatisfied with the placement.
5. Let parents know that you plan to review all placements annually. There may be some children who do not do well in a particular classroom, but may thrive in another setting. Parents and children may be reticent about wanting a change, but need one nonetheless.

If a Parent Opposes the Multiyear Program

There are times when parents will oppose a multiyear placement for their child. Here are some of the reasons:

1. Occasionally a single mother will request a male teacher for her child, to provide a male role model.
2. Some parents want their child with a particular teacher who has a talent for teaching art, music, PE, or other specific subjects.
3. Some parents want their child to experience a variety of different adults.
4. Some parents want to remove their child from the influence of a particular classmate (a bully, for instance).
5. Some parents want traditional educational structures ("If it was good enough for me . . . ").
6. Some parents are afraid their child will get too attached to one teacher.
7. If there are a high number of special-needs students in a particular class, some parents may perceive the class as a "special ed" class.
8. Some parents may just plain not like the teacher.

Whatever the reason for the parents' opposition to the multiyear placement, if it cannot be resolved to their satisfaction, another placement should be considered for the child, if one is available.

Maintaining a Good Relationship

The looping relationship itself seems to foster a much stronger, more positive relationship between parent and teacher, as many teachers have attested; but those teachers also work at maintaining good parent-teacher communications. One third- and fourth-grade teacher, Glenn Killough of Joseph Finberg Elementary School in Attleboro, Massachusetts, has actively worked for many years at cultivating the trust of his students' parents. Read a summery of his views on the subject in "Developing Good Relationships With Parents — 'They Know Where I'm Coming From,' " next page.

The late Dr. Ernest Boyer recognized the vital role that parents play in their children's education in his book, *The Basic School: A Community for Learning*. An excerpt of his book gives some tips for how to make parents feel welcome in today's schools. See "Parents As Partners," page 75.

Keeping A Finger on the Pulse

Schools who institute looping and other reforms need a way to measure their impact on their students and the students' parents. Parent surveys are a common method of gathering information on how a school's program is faring.

Karen Rettig, a first- and second-grade looping teacher at Liberty Center Elementary School in Liberty Center, Ohio, has written "Including Parents in the Process," (page 81) which gives an overview of the beginning of the program, and the methods her school used to communicate with parents at all steps in the process. She includes the results of a parent survey conducted by her school.

Developing Good Relationships
With Parents — "They Know Where I'm Coming From"

Glenn Killough, who is finishing up the second year of a third/fourth grade loop, has always been very big on having strong relationships with his students and their parents.

"Every year I have my own 'meet me' kind of night outside of the normal schedule; I invite the parents to the school, and say, 'Okay, this is me; this is what I'm going to do.' I want to be very approachable. That way, if there's a problem, the parents have already met me. They know that I have no hidden agendas, there are no facades; what they see is what they get."

Killough grew up in Attleboro, went to school there, and considers himself a "blue collar kind of guy" in what is primarily a blue-collar town. He feels the parents know that he is their biggest advocate at the school, and that his intentions are to make them feel as secure as possible.

"They know that if everything's going well I'm going to tell them; and if things aren't going well, they're going to hear it," Killough said.

He wants parents to be as involved as they possibly can, and he's had some impressive success in that regard. His parents regularly volunteer their time and materials to the class, and participate enthusiastically in events. During last summer's class trip to the Boston Museum of Science, he had almost as many parents sign up as students; some of the parents even took a day off from work to go.

"Moms *and* Dads," Killough said. "One of the benefits of being a male in a female-dominated profession is that you get a lot more dads involved."

A Kid's Eye View

Glenn Killough's kids like him as much as his parents do. When asked if they had anything to say about the multiyear assignment, almost every hand in the room shot up, and the students volunteered a flood of testimonials, about both the multiyear concept and Mr. Killough himself. One girl named Dillon said that having the same teacher for two years was "easy, because we had Mr. Killough last year, and we know all his soft spots; so if we want something, all we've got to do is ask him."

Jason felt it was "very cool—even though he gives us harder and harder stuff, because he's had us for two years." Jason said Mr. Killough gives them a lot of fun stuff too, like charting baseball teams; according to Cory, he has "cool pets—tarantulas and cockroaches and stuff." Anthony thinks Mr. Killough is "funny, and makes school sort of fun; he makes it easy." But, "he gives a lot of tests and stuff."

A lot of the kids like Mr. Killough "because he makes us work hard. He pushes us, but he makes it up with lots of good jokes." And one girl, Angela, summed it up for the whole class: "Mr. Killough would never ever let us down."

Joseph Finberg Elementary School

1125 South Main Street
Attleboro, Massachusetts 02703

Phone: 508-222-0535
FAX: 508-223-1584

Looping grades: 1-2
                3-4

Open to visitors: yes

Contact: Ken Cabral, Principal
            Glenn Killough,
            3-4 Teacher

KILLOUGH'S ISLAND

Glenn Killough's fourth-grade class is about to embark on an island adventure — but first they have to build the island.

Killough has been reading C.S. Lewis' *The Chronicles Of Narnia* to the students; now he's having them design and build a model island. He's given them some very specific geographical features that have to be included — but there's a catch. The island also has to be accurate in terms of a scenario that the class will write, based on the characters in *The Chronicles*, that will allow the characters to have an adventure on the island. It will be interesting to see what they come up with — tarantulas, maybe, and cockroaches — and lots of good jokes.

Killough as Parent—Some Concerns

Killough supports the multiyear assignment concept strongly—through the sixth grade. He's not as excited about the practice for seventh and eighth graders.

"I've gone through this as a parent, and I personally don't think it's effective after sixth grade," Killough said. He voiced concerns about the social and emotional needs of junior high students, saying that junior high kids tended to be "cliquey", and that they needed movement, to change classes and rotate teachers, which doesn't happen in Attleboro under the present team teaching structure at the middle school level. "Right now, junior high students only have two teachers for seventh and eighth grades."

Another concern he has, is that he feels junior high students should be exposed to teachers who are specialists in their subjects. "A lot of the middle school teachers aren't specialists, and when you're getting students ready for high school math and science, they really need someone with a strong background in specific subjects."

Killough isn't the only parent who feels this way; a number of parents have voiced the similar concerns. (See *"The Multiyear Assignment: Good for Kids, a Challenge for Teachers,"* page 28. For another viewpoint, see *"The Benefits of Multiyear Teams — Self-Esteem and a Sense of Responsibility and Community,"* on page 95.)

Parents as Partners
by Ernest L. Boyer

The following is an excerpt from the chapter, "Parents as Partners," from the book, *The Basic School: A Community for Learning.*

School-Entry Partnership

One warm September morning, on the first day of school, we visited an elementary school on the outskirts of a large midwestern city. About twenty-eight five-year-olds had congregated outside the door of a kindergarten classroom. Most had walked to school with a parent, guardian or older sibling. A few had come alone. When the bell rang, the teacher invited the children inside, gave each one a smiling-face nametag, and asked them to form a circle on the floor. After a few reassuring hugs, most parents left. Several entered the classroom, but after standing awkwardly on the edges for several minutes, they too drifted away.

The First Day of School

In the Basic School, the first day of school is a time for bonding, not of separation. Rather than forming a circle on the edges, parents are invited to the center and formally welcomed into the community of learning. Specifically, we recommend that each Basic School have a carefully planned first day of school ceremony, a time when parents and guardians and new students join in celebration, greeted by the principal, teachers, and even, perhaps, school board members. On this celebrative occasion, goals can be discussed, a tour offered, refreshments served. Each new parent and student should be teamed up with a parent and student already enrolled in the school.

We recommend, further, that the first day of school be recognized *nationally* as a day of celebration. For this to be accomplished, we suggest that employers give parents released time to join their children at school. After all, workers are given time off to vote and serve on jury duty. Why not give mothers and fathers time off, with pay, to accompany their child to school? Such a move would say to children that education is indeed a partnership between the home and school.

In Massachusetts, Gov. William F. Weld granted state employees released time "to visit classroom teachers, to volunteer in schools, and to serve in school governance." He also asked other employers to provide time for such activities, beginning at the start of each school year. "I have challenged business to redefine the model of what constitutes good corporate citizenship," he added.[1]

In Cleveland, Ohio, parents, grandparents, and guardians are invited to school for what's called Family Day. To promote participation, over one hundred area employers gave fourteen thousand workers paid time off so parents and others could participate. Family Day is now an annual affair, and the number of participating parents, with employer support, keeps growing. According to Michael Charney, a teacher at Lincoln School in Cleveland, "Family Days are a way to move beyond the hope for parental involvement to signaling, in a concrete way, the parent's place in the school."[2] We're suggesting that the first day of school might be considered "Family Day" in communities all across the nation.

On opening day in Japan, the whole school welcomes first-graders and their families. Children, parents, and grandparents dress in their best clothes, with grandmothers in kimonos.

The principal greets the assembly, introduces staff, and talks about school goals. A local town official may speak, lending a community presence. Finally, teachers take students to their rooms, show them their desks, and tell them about procedures. "The total effect of everything is a welcome into a new family," according to author Merry White. "The school is always called 'our' school." [3]

Covenant for Learning

To formalize the home-school partnership, Basic School teachers and parents may wish to enter into a *covenant for learning* at the beginning of the year. By "covenant" we do not mean a formal contract. Rather, we mean a pledge by both partners to participate in the child's learning. Parents might agree, for example, to help the child get to school on time, read to the child, assist with homework, and attend parent-teacher conferences. The school, in turn, might pledge to have clear goals, evaluate carefully the child's progress, and communicate regularly with parents.

Printed as a scroll or certificate, a covenant for learning could be signed as part of the "First Day of School Celebration." Or it could be sent to parents before the start of the school year, and then collected at the ceremonies on opening day. Signing a covenant is, of course, a symbolic act, but if parents and schools would *together* make a cooperative pledge to serve children, the impact would be substantial. Pascal D. Forgione, Delaware's State School Superintendent, put the challenge this way: "Every school should sit down with parents at the beginning of the school year. Let's get parents involved in understanding the criteria and the quality of work at the very beginning."

St. Ann's School in Somerville, Massachusetts, involves all families in a covenant with the school. Each student and parent, with the teacher, pledges to form a partnership for learning. In Grandview, Missouri, parents pledge, in a learning covenant, to set aside at least twenty minutes each night to help their children with schoolwork. They agree, as well, to attend instructional lessons about the school's reading and math programs.

Reading, Ohio, has a citywide covenant for learning which lists responsibilities not just for parents, but for the *entire* community. "All of this has served to focus on the value of education," says John Varis, Reading's superintendent. "What we have behind us now is the power of everyone in the community thinking about education." [4]

Minneapolis, Minnesota, also introduced a citywide pledge. "The Minneapolis Covenant" includes everyone, from school board members to students. Students pledge to attend school regularly, ask for help, respect other students and adults, and keep the school safe. Parents pledge to help their children attend school on time, keep high expectations, communicate regularly with school staff, and provide a quiet space for homework. School staff, in turn, promise, among other things, to set high expectations, respect cultural differences, and "show that I care about all students." [5]

Student Inventory

At the beginning of the school year, all parents surely must become well informed about the school. It is equally important, however, that the school become knowledgeable about the child. [6] We propose, specifically, a *student inventory* for every Basic School, a simple form that would provide a portrait of each student, with such information as a list of favorite books, toys, and songs, as well as learning milestones, including speech development, and early attempts at drawing and writing. [7]

The child's health history could be recorded, too, with such basics as height, weight, and immunizations, and special medication needs. Once established, the student inventory might be passed along from grade to grade, or follow the child who moves to another school. Confidential information is not what we are talking about. Privacy must be protected. It does seem reasonable, however, for schools to gather basic information about the background and interests of each student, to support learning.

The Forest Park Elementary School in St. Paul, Minnesota, recently began asking parents to list their child's interests and strengths, along with the parents' own goals for their child. The information is then used to develop a Parent-Student-Teacher Plan at the beginning of the school year. The plan is helpful during parent conferences in monitoring how effectively school goals are being met. Such a procedure seems appropriate for every school.

Sustaining the Partnership

In the Basic School, the partnership is sustained throughout the year as parents participate in regularly scheduled conferences, as well as informal conversations.[8] Currently, most parents of elementary school children meet with teachers only one to three times a year, according to our survey. Only 10 percent meet as often as once a month (table 1).

TABLE 1	
HOW OFTEN DURING THE COURSE OF THE YEAR DO YOU HAVE A FACE-TO-FACE DISCUSSION ABOUT YOUR CHILD'S WEAKNESSES AND STRENGTHS WITH YOUR CHILD'S TEACHER?	
	PERCENTAGE OF PARENTS AGREEING
More than once a month	5%
About once a month	10
One to three times a year	79
Never	6
SOURCE: THE CARNEGIE FOUNDATION FOR THE ADVANCEMENT OF TEACHING AND THE GEORGE H. GALLUP INTERNATIONAL INSTITUTE, THE INTERNATIONAL SCHOOLING PROJECT, 1994 (UNITED STATES)	

Parent Conferences

We recommend at least four formal parent-teacher meetings annually, and ideally, interaction between the home and school is far more frequent.

Centennial Elementary School in Tucson, Arizona, sends home weekly homework packets for students in early grades, and nightly booklets for student in grades two through five. The school publishes a monthly newsletter with helpful hints for learning and reading at home. Centennial also has an interpreter attend conferences for non-English-speaking parents. [9]

At Westwood Elementary School in Santa Clara, California, a packet of information is sent home to parents every Wednesday, with progress reports, homework assignments, and work samples. "I look forward to Wednesday as my homework day," said one parent. "I spend two hours going through the three envelopes for my three children, but it is time well spent." Adds another parent: "I very much appreciate the large envelope that comes home each Wednesday. It's an easy way to communicate thoughts and opinions back to teachers." Notes a third parent: "The envelope reminds students that parents know what homework is expected. It makes shirking it a little harder! The weekly communication promotes an all-around unity for child, parent and the school." [10]

Such intimate interaction between the home and school means adding even more responsibility to a teacher's already overburdened schedule. To provide additional support,

Basic Schools may wish to use teacher aides, volunteers from the local university, senior citizens, and even high school students to help out. Teachers simply cannot do it all.

A Parent Place

We also recommend that each Basic School have a parent place, a comfortable location in the building where parents gather throughout the day and mingle, informally, with staff or other parents. [11] In schools where space is tight, chairs might be arranged at the end of a corridor, or near the school office, or a corner in the library might become "the parent place," sending a strong signal to parents that they are considered full members of the school "family."

While visiting an elementary school in the West, we came across a "parent center" that housed, along with a coffee pot and homey furniture, a library of parenting books, tips on how to make a neighborhood walk educational for children, and samples of new children's literature. In another school, we found a "grandparents corner" in the library, with a big rocking chair and a selection of books close by. Every Basic School could create such a place for parents — and grandparents.

Parent Inventory

Each group of parents has a substantial talent that can enrich the social and educational program of a school in a variety of ways. Therefore, we recommend that every Basic School conduct an inventory to identify the skills and experience parents have and the kind of volunteer work they might wish to do. Such information could include artistic talent, construction skills, special knowledge acquired from world travels, and interesting hobbies, all of which could enrich the school.

Orchard School in Ridgewood, New Jersey, put together an "Encyclopedia of People" that listed parents' interests. On any given day, mothers and fathers can be seen working in the library, giving classroom talks about their jobs, or serving with art consultants. Orchard School parents have worked with art teacher Tom Wallace to produce a school calendar that features children's drawings. Parents recently spent weekends working side by side with the principal and teachers, raising money to build a new playground and obtaining the necessary permits.

At Dover Elementary School in Westlake, Ohio, parents run a "book publishing center," binding as many as one thousand books a month—books written and illustrated by the students. At Manhattan's Public School 111, parents established English courses for Spanish-speaking parents. And parents at the Fairfax Elementary School in Cleveland built a new play-and-learn facility on the school grounds, with a kindergarten play lot and nature study area.

Again, employers can help promote such participation. State Farm Insurance in Bloomington, Illinois, for example, recently announced it would give its sixty-seven thousand employees paid time off to volunteer in schools. [12] North Carolina National Bank gives employees two hours of paid leave each week to participate in school activities or confer with teachers. The bank also matches, dollar for dollar, an employee's financial contribution to his or her child's school. "Successful parenting is as challenging as successful banking," says one official. [13]

Several years ago, *Hemmings Motor News* began "education participation days." Employees have two days off each year to visit schools, participate in volunteer activities, or observe classes. The program did not evolve from employee pressures; rather, it was initiated by the owners and manager who made a commitment to family-friendly policies. [14]

The State of California recently passed an initiative called "The Family-School Partnership Act," which allows parents to take off eight hours a month, or up to forty hours each school year, with employer support. "No single factor can impact our children and our schools more positively than parent involvement," says Delaine Eastin, California State Superintendent of Public Instruction. [15]

Parent Coordinators

Finally, each Basic School should, we believe, have a *parent coordinator*, someone specifically designated to lead the home partnership program — greeting parents when they come to school, organizing parent education workshops, helping teachers with voice-mail messages, operating homework hotlines, and arranging home visits. The coordinator could be a parent volunteer, a senior citizen, or a college student fulfilling a commitment to a community service program.

Lowery Elementary School in Houston, Texas, uses a parent coordinator to recruit and work with parent volunteers, with remarkable results. More than six hundred parents now work in twenty-six volunteer programs, logging 13,500 hours of service every year.

Whitcomb Elementary School in Richmond, Virginia, has a paid parent coordinator who schedules "Let's Talk" sessions every Thursday morning. There's a "Coffee with the Principal" meeting once a month. [16] At Public School 199 in Manhattan, the parent coordinator is a teacher who conducts Tuesday evening discussion groups on subjects ranging from "whole language" instruction to home science projects. [17]

Jackson-Keller Elementary School in San Antonio, Texas, is located in a neighborhood with a highly mobile population, surrounded by housing developments and apartments, with many single-parent families. A few years ago, parents were not involved in the school. But the principal, Alicia Thomas, joined by teachers and the children, hosted "Donuts for Dads" and "Muffins for Moms" parties on Saturday mornings in the lobbies of apartments close by. Barriers were broken. Trust was built. Parents became partners. Teachers felt supported. Children were the winners.

The message is clear. It is simply impossible to have an island of excellence in a sea of community indifference, and when parents become school partners, the results can be consequential and enduring.

Notes:

1. Ken Plumley, personal communication, Office of the Governor, Springfield, MA, 7 February 1995; see also remarks as delivered by Gov. William Weld before the Committee on Educational Policy, Worcester, MA, 24 October 1991.

2. Michael Charney and Cleveland Teachers Union, personal communication, 3 February 1995; see also Michael Charney, "Parent Involvement in Cleveland," *Rethinking Schools* 7, no. 3 (spring 1993), 5.

3. Merry White, *The Japanese Educational Challenge: A Commitment to Children* (New York: The Free Press, 1987), 111.

4. John Varis, personal communication, April 1995; see also materials from Reading Board of Education, Reading, OH, including "Reading Community Schools Memorandum of Understanding, 1992-93."

5. Kevin Duchschere, "Kids, Parents, School Officials All Cross Their Hearts at Rally," *Minneapolis Star Tribune*, 21 January 1994; and Minneapolis Public Schools, press release, 20 January 1994.

6. Researchers have found that the majority of school districts do not have any activities or programs to ease the transition of youngsters from preschool experiences to kindergartem. RMC Research Corp., "Transitions to Kindergarten in American Schools," report funded by the U.S. Department of Education, Office of Policy and Planning, 1992; in "Report Says Few Schools Promote Preschool-to-School Transition," *Report on Preschool Programs*, 6 May 1992, 91-92, and Deborah L. Cohen, "Study Finds Little Done to Ease Transition to School," *Education Week*, 22 April 1992, 4.

7. The student inventory we suggest is based on our analysis of parent entry forms and parent enrollment forms in thirty-five randomly selected elementary schools in ten states throughout the country. We discovered that most merely asked for basic health statistics. The only national form was the computerized one formerly used by the federally funded national Migrant Student Record Transfer System, based in Arkansas, that tracked the two million school children migrating seasonally across the United States. A few states are currently exploring a computerized form for their students as well.

8. Parents who receive frequent and positive messages from teachers tend to get more involved in their children's education than parents who do not receive such communications; Carole Ames, Madhab Khoju, and Thomas Watkins, *Parent Involvement: The Relationship Between School-to-Home Communication and Parents' Perceptions and Beliefs*, Center on Families, Communities, Schools, and Children's Learning, The Johns Hopkins University, Baltimore, MD, Report No.15, March 1993.

9. Denise Lunsford, personal communication, 6 March 1995; see also nomination forms, 1993-94 Elementary Blue Ribbon Schools Program, sponsored by the U.S. Department of Education.

10. Joya Chatterjee, personal communication, 7 March 1995; see also nomination forms, 1993-94 Elementary Blue Ribbon Schools Program, sponsored by the U.S. Department of Education.

11. Vivian R. Johnson, Parent/Family Centers: Dimensions of Functioning in 28 Schools in 14 States, Center on Families, Communities, Schools, and Children's Learning, The Johns Hopkins University, Baltimore, MD, report no. 20, September 1993.

12. David Burke, personal communication, 7 March 1995; also State Farm Insurance Company, "State Farm Offers Employees Paid Time Off to Help in Schools," press release, Bloomington, IL, 7 February 1995.

13. Boyer, *Ready to Learn*, 73, citing Hal Morgan and Kerry Tucker, *Companies That Care* (New York: Simon and Schuster, 1991), 330-31, and Sandra Conway, NCNB, November, 1991.

14. Charles Waters, *Hemmings Motor News*, personal communication, April 1995; and Boyer, Ready to Learn, 73-74.

15. California Department of Education, "New Law Allows Working Parents to Take Time Off to Help in Their Children's Schools," press release, 3 February 1995.

16. Southern Education Foundation, Inc., "Getting Involved: One Parent's Story," SEF News 7, no. 1, Atlanta, GA. February 1993, 7-8.

17. Susan R. Larabee, parent, personal communication, 10 August 1995.

Looping at Liberty Center Elementary School — Including Parents in the Process

by Karen Rettig

Making the Decision

"You want me to do what? Keep my children for how long?"

It was my sixth year of teaching, and I had begun to feel stagnant. My principal at the time had denied an earlier request to change grade levels. He suggested, however, a viable alternative—looping. Looping, he explained, is the process of keeping a group of children together with the same teacher for two academic years. He pointed out that I would be changing grade levels as I had originally requested. It wasn't quite what I had in mind, but I suppose I had asked for it.

Doing the Research

I was ready for a change. The idea of looping, however, raised new questions and concerns, such as: how do I handle the same child for two years? how do I go about developing an additional year of curriculum? how do I deal with special-needs children? Fortunately, my principal provided time for a slow transition.

Over a two-year period, we read literature, attended workshops and seminars, and visited schools with similar programs. Prior to a visit to Kentucky, still unsure, I was prepared to tell my principal, "No!" I felt the change was too drastic for me. Only after I spoke to veteran teachers in Kentucky, who encouraged me with stories about the benefits of looping, did I say "yes."

Offering Parents a Choice

The proper development of the program was a challenge for us, since looping was a relatively new concept. We created our own standards and guidelines to fit the specific needs of our staff and children. Although any two-year combination would work, we decided to begin with two looping first grades and one traditional single-grade first grade. We offered the parents a choice of placing their children in the traditional classroom or a looping classroom.

We began by sending parents an informational letter followed by a looping handbook which described the program, its advantages, disadvantages, and general procedures. We then held a meeting with the parents, teachers and administrators, and gave everyone a change to voice concerns, get questions answered, and alleviate anxieties.

Much to our surprise, parents were excited, understood the advantages of a looping program, and wanted their children to participate. We were actually unable to accommodate all parents who requested their children be a part of the program.

Liberty Center Elementary School

P.O. Box 434
Liberty Center, OH 43532

Phone: 419-533-5011
FAX: 419-533-5036

Looping grades: 1-2

Open to visitors: Yes

Contact: Karen Rettig

Ongoing Communication

We communicated with our parents on a regular basis through a weekly newsletter, and sent home a calendar of summer projects that parents could do with their children at the end of the first year (see Summer Projects, page 122).

Parents consistently reported the positive effects looping was having on their children: a lack of anxiety about beginning second grade, a lack of stomachaches, more sociability, and so on.

The Parent Survey

At the end of the two-year cycle, we sent surveys home for parents to fill out, which provided a lot of valuable and overwhelmingly positive feedback on the looping program (see below). We tallied the answers, and informed parents of the results of the survey.

A Final Picnic

To provide some closure for the program, we invited parents to school for a picnic, where I chatted with them as we watched the children play. The shy, introverted child who didn't seem to have a friend two years ago skipped and sang with two friends. The contemptible, friendless class bully played soccer with a group. He insisted that the others play fair or not play at all. The "clique" forgot what the old quarrels were about; they just wanted to hold onto one another and not let go.

So did I. The social and emotional growth evident in everyone that afternoon — children, parents, and teachers—assured me, and the parents, that looping was the right decision.

We were all ready to face the next challenge — a discussion of third-fourth grade looping.

Looping

PARENT SURVEY   Liberty Center Elementary School

[*Editor's note: This represents a tally of all completed survey forms received from parents, plus a sampling of their individual comments.*]

Directions: Please read each of the questions and rank them according to the chart below. Please feel free to make additional comments on the lines provided.

> 1. agree   2. neutral   3. disagree

I. General Questions

A. Would you place your child in the looping program again?
>31 agree   2 neutral   0 disagree

B. Do you feel the looping program made your child feel more comfortable with school in general?
>30 agree   3 neutral   0 disagree

Comments:
• *Absolutely!*
• *Yes — he commented many times how glad he was to keep the same teacher.*

C. Do you feel your child missed out on having a new teacher, new experiences and/or new friends?

3 agree   11 neutral   19 disagree

Comments:
- *Maybe? (new friends underlined).*
- *Especially the first years I feel he was very comfortable and secure in a familiar atmosphere.*

II. Academics

A. Do you feel your child has benefited academically because of the looping program?

29 agree   4 neutral   0 disagree

Comments:
- *Yes!*
- *When they are happy and comfortable they are much more likely to do well.*
- *He works well with his teacher and that in itself is an academic benefit because he wants to please her.*

B. Do you feel your child was academically challenged by staying with the same teacher for two years?

23 agree   10 neutral   0 disagree

Comments:
- *Yes!*
- *I think he has an excellent teacher and she has done well to challenge them at their own level; the looping program probably enhanced this as the teacher was familiar with each student.*
- *She knew from the start what he is capable of and in what areas he needs to focus. In fact, when they change teachers, I think they should have individual reports on each student, i.e., strong and weak points.*

III. Social

A. Do you like having your child with the same group of children for two years?

15 agree   10 neutral   3 disagree

Comments:
- *I think it made Katie feel comfortable.*
- *Some were a plus—others were not! But there are always situations like that.*
- *A lot of socialization takes place during recess, lunch, and extracurricular activities.*

B. Did your child like being with the same group of friends for two years?

24 agree   5 neutral   3 disagree

Comments:
- *She didn't seem to mind.*
- *He says yes.*

C. Do you feel your child's friendships are limited because of the looping program?

        5 agree   10 neutral   18 disagree

Comments:
- *She still had friends from the other classes, too.*
- *There is always lunch and recesses for them to take advantage of meeting new friends. And Bruce has.*
- *There are kids in the other classes that he associates with outside of school.*

D. Do you think "cliques" were formed because of the looping program?

        8 agree   4 neutral   21 disagree

Comments:
- *Yes, but you'd have them anyway.*
- *Probably better and closer friendships.*

E. Are "cliques" formed regardless of the looping program?

        29 agree   3 neutral   1 disagree

Comments:
- *Absolutely.*

F. Do you feel the looping program established better discipline routines?

        23 agree   8 neutral   0 disagree

Comments:
- *I have no real experience with the discipline end of things. Fortunately our son hasn't had any trouble here.*
- *The teacher knows from the start of year two who needs stronger discipline techniques.*
- *Absolutely, the teacher knows eachchild better and how to discipline that child.*

IV. Program

A. Would you recommend this program to a parent of a new first grade student?

        31 agree   4 neutral   0 disagree

[Comments:
- *In fact — can Maxwell be in this program? Can I request Mrs. Rettig for him also? . . . She's great!*
- *We already have been.*

B. Would you like your child to be involved in a third-fourth grade loop?

        20 agree   13 neutral   0 disagree

Comments:
- *So does he.*
- *Depends on who the teachers are. The teacher makes or breaks the looping program. So far the teachers selected have been great! (I really feel this is important. To be honest, there are certain teachers I would not want my child to have for one year, let alone two!*

C. If the majority of the responses are interested in continuing the looping program, should the entire grade level loop? (No traditional classrooms)

        12 agree   11 neutral   8 disagree

Comments:
- *If there are those that don't like it or don't want to try it, they should have an alternative option.*
- *I think the parents should be able to choose what is right for their child.*
- *I think that if some parents disagree that there should be an alternative available if possible.*

D. Do you see a need to "remix" the current looping students before entering a third-fourth grade loop?

     23 agree   6 neutral   4 disagree

Comments:
- *I say it may be a good idea, [but] the student wants the same kids in class.*
- *I think friendships would be too "rooted" [otherwise]. They are too young for that.*
- *I think it would be good if they didn't [remix].*

V. Parent Thoughts

A. What advantages did you see with the looping program?
1. Comfortability
2. Academic awareness

B. What disadvantages did you see with the looping program?
1. None
2. If they didn't get along with the teacher or other students

C. Additional comments [overview]:
1. Concerns over teacher assignments for the third-fourth grade loop
2. Possible conflicts with student to student relationships
3. Possible conflicts with student to teacher relationships

D. Additional individual comments:
- *I think the program is very beneficial, especially the second year; when most teachers are getting to know their students, the looping teachers are picking up where they left off the previous year.*
 [Note from Karen Rettig — This woman's daughter is a "shy" child to the point of tears and stomachaches.]
- *I think having the same teacher can be a very beneficial thing for the student. On arrival of the second year there is less anxiety because they already know their teacher and what is expected of them. They can "get into the business" of learning that much quicker. It was wonderful sending our son to school on the first day of his second year because he was so eager to see his teachers and classmates. No stomachaches or fear thinking — what will my teacher be like, etc.*
 [Note from Mrs. Rettig: Bruce is an "introverted" child. Two years gave him confidence to speak out.]
- *There wasn't any fear about returning the second year — same teacher, same students. Things were familiar. The students should mix with the other classes, not just the same 25 all day, every day . (Have art, music, or gym together.)*

CHAPTER 5

Flexibility is the Key
Multiyear Teaming

In the five years that Cyril K. Brennan Middle School has participated in multiyear teaching assignments, principal Frank Leary has noticed a marked increase in the cooperative spirit of the school's teachers.

"Teachers now share more," Leary said; "and it's not just materials; it's ideas, it's thoughts. It's what we call the big pieces."

The teachers at Brennan are part of two- and sometimes three-person teams who teach grades 5-6 and 7-8 in two-year teaching assignments. The school is on its third group of students experiencing the two-year assignments, which means some of the teaching teams are at the beginning of their third multiyear assignment. Leary says that over 90 percent of the teachers are enthusiastic about the multiyear concept.

"They find that it provides the students with an opportunity for ongoing learning and ongoing progress; the teachers don't have to spend the months of September and October setting up parameters for what their expectations are each year. They don't have to do a lot of assessment during those months, either, to find out where the students are functioning academically.

"The two-year assignment is where you really get to learn about kids and you," said Leary. "Middle school is a great time of exploration; it's like a great voyage you're on. It's an exciting voyage, because these years are so exciting to be with these kids, and you have to be very energized. They're very demanding; and it's like you're in a tennis match, and you get caught up in the pulse of the game.

"What I see is teachers performing at a very high level of competency; and they teach kids rather than teach content," Leary said.

Ongoing Mentoring Program

Brennan participates in a mentorship program with Texas Instruments that is five years old—as old as the multiyear structure in the school. Part of the mentorship program involves providing teachers with inservice training. The 1995-96 school year included the training of 20 staff members on the subject of diversity, which is relevant to Brennan as a multicultural school.

Texas Instraments works with both teachers and students. The mentors follow the students from the time they enter seventh grade all the way through eighth grade, just like the classroom teachers do. "I think it's the two-year assignment that makes the mentorship program work so well," said Leary.

The mentorship program is sponsored by the Women's Initiative of Texas Instruments, and among other things deals with gender issues, including some of the current research on how boys and girls learn differently. The initiative provides professional role models for both young men and women in such areas as marketing, quality control, personnel services, and engineering. Most of the women from TI have masters' degrees; many of them are in engineering research.

Teachers and Students — a Powerful Team

Each team at Brennan is made up of either two or three teachers and, in the case of two-person teams, between 50 and 60 students. Inclusion teams have a lower teacher-student ratio—generally between 32 and 40 students, not more than a third of whom will be special-needs students. Inclusion teams are supported by a teacher's aide, or ILA; additionally, one of the teachers on each inclusion team is special-ed certified.

The students in each team make up a code of ethics, or code of conduct, for themselves, and have team meetings to discuss issues.

Leary explained how the team approach can work. "If the teachers are with a group of kids, and one of the kids comes into class and says, 'Someone's taken my calculator,' the teachers know that this is a very big deal for this student. They're likely to stop and have a team meeting at that time, and conduct an open forum — which represents what government is all about—with the kids who discuss what happened. 'Did someone misplace it? Is it in someone's book bag? Did it go in here? Did we put it in the wrong place?'

"Usually you eliminate a lot of those issues that start out small, and become huge, that were not dealt with when teachers had the students for one year, and possibly for one period out of a seven-period day — 'I'm sorry you lost your books, but I've got another hundred kids coming in here right now.' When you deal with smaller units of kids you can deal with those issues."

Teaming Provides Flexibility

The two- or three-person teaching team is made up of teachers with different strengths to bring to the partnership. Most of the time, with a two-person team, one member of the team is skilled in math and science, the other in language arts and social studies, although occasionally another combination will be created — for instance, a science/language arts person teamed with a math/social studies person. Once the team is created, it is given enormous latitude, both in the way the members divide up the teaching responsibilities, and in the way they divide up instructional time. Each team is different; one team, for instance (see "Kindred Spirits" page 91) has both teachers and an instructional aide with the whole class during social studies, while dividing the class up at other times for math, science and language arts instruction.

Flexibility is the mantra at Cyril K. Brennan. The administration provides the teaching teams with a schedule that blocks out periods when the students are with specialists — art, music, P.E., etc.; this time becomes the teaching team's planning time. The rest of the time the team can structure as it sees fit.

"We try to give our teachers large blocks of instructional time," Leary said.

One advantage of the team structure at Brennan is that the teams are able to use various grouping strategies throughout the day as their students' needs necessitate — grouping strategies that are generally reserved for the lower grades. Teachers may design cooperative learning strategies for part of the day, and skills-based small group sessions at other times of the day. "It meets a lot of different needs," Leary said.

"I think that in middle school the more groupings you have, the better off you are," he continued. "Kids become much more flexible; they become much better problem solvers. And it's not always the A kids over here and the B kids over there, in a homogeneous situation." In this type of arrangement, also, remediation can be accomplished when needed in a much more natural setting—important for middle-schoolers whose self-esteem is on the line.

Transitions — Coming to Brennan . . .

A lot of attention is paid to students' transitions in and out of Brennan. Fourth-grade students from the two main schools that feed Brennan visit the middle school near the end of their school year. The principal also goes to visit the fourth graders, who have brainstormed questions to ask him. Parents' nights are scheduled, one at the elementary schools, then one at the middle school after the fourth-graders students have visited the school. "The parents have a chance to dialogue some of the information that they and their kids have received, and then ask any questions they felt were not answered or covered. We give them a tour of the building that night and then we have a question and answer period," Leary said.

Articulation sheets are done on outgoing fourth grade students for their fifth grade teachers, providing information like what the students have been studying, what types of reading they've been doing, and so on.

"We always try to get information on individual students about what they do, what they do well, whether they function well in a small group, whether they work well in a buddy system, can they do things individually, do they need more structure, are they visual learners?"said Leary. Articulation sheets are also done between sixth and seventh grades, which ends up putting quite a demand on the sixth-grade teachers.

"Our sixth grade teachers are getting ready to move back down to fifth grade, so they're accepting new fifth graders while they're giving away sixth graders; they end up really inundated with articulation."

The district is working on a portfolio assessment process which will involve students at the end of a two-year assignment taking their portfolios to their new teachers, and being interviewed by those teachers about the work they've been doing. It has begun in the lower grades, but will take time to get up through the grades.

. . . And Moving On

Students nearing the end of eighth grade begin to prepare for their entrance into high school. The process is similar in some ways to the students' entry in fifth grade; the high school principal comes to Brennan for a visit, then the middle school students visit the high school, and discuss curriculum issues. All eighth graders are given a writing test and an algebra test; students recommended for English and science honors courses are tested individually. At least one, and sometimes two, parents' nights take place.

"Brennan communicates with the high school on all our special ed kids, and on those kids who are not special ed but may need monitoring as they go into high school," said Leary; "— kind of a cadre of special ed kids and high-risk kids. We communicate about who they are, what might be their concerns; we talk about anything from absenteeism to bilingualism to students not proficient in English, to kids who are gifted."

Cyril K. Brennan Middle School

135 County Road
Attleboro, Massachusetts 02703

Phone: 508-223-1550
FAX: 508-223-1555

Looping grades: 5-6
                7-8

Open to visitors: Yes

Contact: Frank Leary, Principal
          Lynne Marcet,
          Kristin Manning,
          5-6 teachers

INCLUSION — A FORMULA FOR SUCCESS

Inclusion = Flexibility

Cyril K. Brennan practices full inclusion for its special-needs students; it does not use pullouts. Students with special needs are dealt with primarily by the classroom teachers (one of whom is always special-ed certified) within the classroom setting.

"We may have three or five kids who are reading three years below grade level, and another group reading two or three level above that; we have skills-based groups deal with that. It's all part of the flexibility," Leary said. When a student does require assistance from an outside specialist (for instance, a Title 1 teacher or speech specialist), the specialist comes into the classroom and deals with the student in what is essentially just another grouping arrangement.

"The more flexibility the team has, the better off we are," Leary said. "The minute you pull somebody out, you lose your flexibility, because every day that John Smith has to go to the resource teacher for a set period, you can't regroup your kids. You can't do a long-term project. It really defeats the purpose of what inclusion should be, which is to keep the kids together. And the flexibility you lose is needed at middle schools."

Teaming + Inclusion = Resources Working Together

With the special ed certification of regular classroom teachers, and with specialists coming into the classroom to deal with kids in their regular setting, the team members and specialists can look at all the kids at the same time and decide what groupings will work for them on that particular day.

"Every teacher's got different strengths and different strategies; the team members can get together and ask, 'Who's got a strategy that will work?' It's a good collaboration," Leary said.

Teaming + Inclusion + Resources = Self-Esteem

Leary sees one of the major purposes of inclusion, especially at the middle-school level, as fostering self-esteem and the ability to be a contributing citizen.

"I think isolation for middle-school kids is the worst; they want to be with their peers. Peer acceptance is very important. It's surprising how kids' opinions change about other kids after they've worked on a project with someone. I've heard kids in the cafeteria say [about a special-needs kid], 'I never knew he could do this; I didn't know he could do this at all.' Special-needs kids have been isolated for so long," Leary said. "Inclusion is much more real-life."

Kindred Spirits

Lynne Marcet and Kristin Manning are finishing up the first year of a two-year assignment that spans grades five and six at Cyril K. Brennan Middle School. They've been together as a team for four years, and have found kindred spirits in each other.

"I think it's worked wonderfully for us, because personally and philosophically, we are very compatible," Lynne Marcet said; "and I think that's an extremely important piece of this whole teaming process.

"Another thing that works very well for us is that we really are able to teach what our skills are; I'm strong in math and science, and Kris is strong in communications, and we're able to really focus in on those areas that we're responsible for, and do a lot more with our students."

"It's happened since we've been together that we've been able to continue to focus in those areas," added Kristin Manning. "Probably had we not been placed in this situation we'd both have to still be teaching all content areas. Lynne tends definitely to be involved more in area workshops and continuing education involving math and science, whereas I have focused more in the communications areas. And that's been something that we have been allowed to do."

While other teams have had more administrative input into how they could divide teaching responsibilities, Marcet and Manning have basically been given the option of making those decisions themselves. "It's really worked well, I think, for us and for the kids," Marcet said.

There are staff development areas that both teachers get involved in; both are participating in a mentorship course right now, as well as a gender equity course; and they're both PALMS [Partnerships Advancing the Learning of Math and Science] certified teachers. PALMS is a statewide initiative to enhance the education of math and science and create a more quality curriculum in those areas. Marcet is actually a PALMS trainer.

"Even though it's funded as a math and science initiative, it deals a lot with philosophy and the way to approach things, so it expands all areas of the curriculum," said Marcet.

"Both of us have some connection in the other areas of the curriculum, too, so we tend to work very closely in terms of overall planning," said Manning. "We are fairly thematic in our approach to teaching, so we do sit down before we approach a unit and determine exactly how we're going to go about working in each of our areas. I very often know exactly what's going on in her area, and vice versa, which keeps things very connected. And we teach social studies together, with the whole class, so that's another piece that is connected."

A Two-Year Approach to Curriculum

During the previous two-year assignment, the team used wellness as an overriding theme for the entire time span, and tied all curriculum areas into that theme. This time they're trying a different approach.

"We've spent a lot of time in this fifth grade trying to build a foundation of process skills. I've done a lot in my classes on the writing process, for example," said Manning; "How to format paragraphs, how to do story mapping. . . ." Manning is presenting these process skills now so that the students will have tools to apply to next year's more content-driven curriculum.

"I think this is the first year that we've had the opportunity to really be able to do that," Manning said; "in working with the first group of kids we still didn't quite know how to approach everything the right way; and the more experience we've gained in working in this type of assignment, the more we can make decisions about what works and what doesn't."

"I think we're at the point now," added Marcet, "that we can say, 'Okay, you how to approach this problem, you know what strategies to use, or skills to use,' and then we can let them go and do it; and the quality of their work is a lot better, because they know the expectations.

"We found ourselves a bit worried at the beginning of the year [January], thinking, 'Gosh, we haven't even done a big project yet, we haven't had parents in for a big parent night to display work,' because there wasn't much of that going on at the beginning of this year; but we've had to remind ourselves of what our whole purpose is in structuring the assignment. I think we'll definitely see the effectiveness of it, as we move on through next year."

One of the deciding factors in this process skills approach is the fact that the fifth-grade class receives students from three different Attleboro primary schools.

"With all the different teachers, and all the different schools, the children are coming from different points; so in order to get them all to the point where we need them to be so that they can move on, we have to spend a lot of time talking about problem-solving strategies, the writing process, science process skills and those kinds of things," Manning said.

Year Two Starts in June — Summer Projects

One practice that has met with a surprising amount of enthusiasm from the students in Manning and Marcet's class is the summer assignment between grades five and six. During the last multiyear assignment, Manning assigned a book review project—the students each had to read a book, report on it, then create a project based on the book. The students also went home for the summer with their portfolios.

"They were able to add to them and work on some of the reflection that we didn't have time to do during the year," Manning said.

In addition, Marcet sent home a calendar with different math and science activities, from which the students had to choose a certain number to do a week. They kept a journal of all the activities that they did, the results, (what happened, why they thought what happened happened), then picked a favorite activity and shared it with the class upon returning in the fall.

To avoid having students show up for class in September without having accomplished anything, Manning and Marcet spelled out consequences for not doing what they were supposed to do—specifically, staying after school to do the work until they caught up. For most of the kids, that wasn't necessary.

"The activities that most of the kids did were incredible," Manning said; "and they were so excited about it. If we hadn't planned on allowing them time to share their projects we would have had to put that in because they were so intent on being able to."

Manning and Marcet ascribe a lot of the students' enthusiasm to the fact that they had a large measure of choice in the activities that they did. "With the calendar I sent home, there was an activity for every day; and they had to do, I think, fifty or so activities throughout; so they had a lot of choice," Marcet said. "And they could also make up their own activities if they wanted to. They could choose any book they wanted to for the book review; so it was something that was of interest to them. And we tend to experiment with things that are more hands-on, which gets them excited. I think that the activities themselves were motivating for them."

Special-Needs Kids Participated Too

Because it's an inclusive setting, the classroom contains kids with abilities that range over a very wide spectrum. The two teachers are finding that their students are very accepting of each other in terms of everyone's ability level.

"Some of the kids came back with their book reviews and had done a very basic read, and still had something to present," said Manning; "and they were very respected for what they had done.

"That still continues to amaze me. I see it every day; we do a lot of sharing in all areas, and the kids are very accepting and respectful of each other and what they have to share."

Saying Goodbye

Letting go is hard at the end of the two-year cycle, for the students and the teachers. It does help that Manning and Marcet get to have a lot of input into what their students' needs are and where they will be placed going into seventh grade. But it's still an emotional time.

"Kids come back to visit," said Marcet. At the beginning of this school year, their previous class did more than that; the students initiated an after-school reunion. Two students had moved away and transferred to different schools; the two kids caught rides and came back to Brennan for the reunion.

The Benefits of Multiyear Teams —
Self-Esteem and a Sense of Responsibility and Community

Mimi Forbes and Dave Cox are sold on two-person multiyear teams. Mimi Forbes is the principal of Robert J. Coelho Middle School; Dave Cox is one member of a two-person teaching team that as of June 1996 was finishing up a seventh/eighth-grade assignment.

Both people have some basis for comparison. Forbes came to Attleboro from the Boston public school system, which did not use the multiyear approach; Cox had taught junior high math for 25 years before becoming a member of his two-person team.

"I've found that the kids in general are better behaved," said Forbes. "I find that the teachers and the children take responsibility for themselves and one another. I was quite taken with what Paulina [one of Cox's eighth grade students] said at a meeting with NELMS [New England League of Middle Schools]. She said that the kids actually learned better how to make friends; they learned what it takes to be a friend; and they learned how to keep friends, because they do it. The skills they learn are really quite valuable; it's like living in a family.

"I think the two-person team in the multiyear assignment is what allows this to happen. The students develop a small-team spirit, and then they develop the community spirit within that."

"I did an observation in a classroom with a team with two teachers; I happened to do the observation on both teachers in the same day," said Forbes; "and I heard the same message from both teachers. I heard, 'Gee, I like your question.' 'Gee, that's a really good question. I'm glad you asked that.' And I heard it from everybody, said in different ways.

"Think about the mindset that kids like this build up over the course of two years; 'I'm valued; I'm important; what I have to say is important; I make a contribution to this class.' I think when you build kids up to realize that and to start to feel how important they are, they make the monumental contributions that you want them to make. So that's really where I've seen wonderful things."

"It works very well," added Cox. "You really do get to know the kids very well. One of the kids got up [at the NELMS meeting] and said, 'Well, sometimes they get to know you too well.' I don't know if that's possible, but you really do know what the kids' strengths and weaknesses are.

"I also know what kind of lesson I'm going to teach next; I know what they're going to like, or not like, so all that helps. Along with the two-person teams.

"It's kind of difficult to teach eighth grade on occasion," Cox said; "Sometimes it may take you at least half the school year to get the kids with the program so that now you can teach. With these kids, on the first day of school, you're right back to teaching again. You know every single kid; they know you; there's no real problem."

Multiyear Teachers Try Harder

According to Cox, the multiyear assignment gives the teacher an incentive to try harder with the kids. "If you only have a kid for one year, or for one class a day, you tend to think, 'Well, maybe I can make it through a year;' but if you're going to have him for two years, you'd better really figure out how to deal with that kid."

The two-person team arrangement helps. Instead of seeing 125 students in a series of 40-minute periods during the course of the day Cox and his teaching partner, Pam Puccio, share their 50 students in various groupings for longer blocks of time, dealing with each student two or three times a day. Cox teaches pre-algebra[1] and science, while Pam teaches communications and social sciences; their students are divided up evenly between them into two home rooms.

"In the past, there were students whose names I might not even be sure of, even towards the end of the year," Cox said.

Advisor/Advisee Relationship — A Natural Outgrowth

"One of the things discussed in middle schools as really important for kids of this age is the whole concept of an advisor/advisee relationship; a student is assigned an advisor and meets with this person forever and ever," said Forbes. "The sole purpose is for the staff to get to know the kids, and for kids to have access to caring adults." Unfortunately, according to Forbes, it's generally a contrived arrangement that doesn't always do what it's supposed to do.

Forbes and Cox believe that the two-person team and the looping arrangement provide the same benefits as a formal advisor/advisee relationship, in a more natural setting.

"What better people for kids to go to than their teachers? With the multiyear assignment you've automatically increased the access to really caring adults, who get to know the kids really well," said Forbes. "With the two-person team and the multiyear arrangement, you don't need the advisor-advisee component," added Cox.

The Result — Well-Adjusted Kids

"I see really well-adjusted kids coming out of this; I see kids who leave here that, for the most part, are fun to be with. There's less of a feeling of us and them, and more of a concept of us," Forbes said. "I think it's minimized our discipline problems."

School Rules, Team Rules

Forbes makes few rules that apply schoolwide — "the normal ones; you can't run in the hall, that sort of thing —;" apart from that, each team of students develops its own rules. "What happens over the period of two years is that the team becomes a community, with its own laws and mores, and you're actually running a school that operates on different guidelines from team to team," Forbes said.

---

[1] The pre-algebra class is actually a grouping of students from all three eighth-grade teams; another teacher teaches algebra, and the third teaches a more basic math course. The students are placed in the classes based on performance on a seventh-grade standardized math test. Cox doesn't like the arrangement, because it limits him and his partner for part of the day in terms of the flexibility of their schedule.

Cox's team doesn't have formal rules. "Our team is called the Expectations Team, because we figure everyone knows how to behave. We tell the kids, 'We expect you to do things that are normal; we expect you to do your work, and if you don't, we'll tell you about it.' "

Committees — A Big Part of the Team Approach

The team has team meetings once a month to discuss various issues; in addition, every student belongs to a committee, and on Tuesdays, they work on their committees for an hour to an hour and a half.

"We have a team recognition committee, that makes up awards for kids on the team who've done different things," said Cox; "We have a birthday committee, that makes up birthday cards for everyone on the team; we have the courtyard committee —"

And then there's the breakfast committee. Once a month, the breakfast committee solicits donations of food from all the team members, then the team puts on a breakfast "with this massive quantity of food," Cox said. The team members invite their parents, or "anybody that wants to show up;" they also invite any guest speakers that have come to the school in the past month or so.

A Sense of Responsibility

"The most incredible thing I've seen," said Forbes, "and I've seen it grow in the past three years, is the responsibility that the children take on." The school recently had an Earth Day celebration in front of the school, and the school's committees planned it, inviting guests from the community and then running the whole event.

"There were almost 700 kids outside, listening to speeches and presentations from a mike that didn't carry, and the kids for the most part were outstanding," Forbes said. There were teachers in the crowd monitoring the kids, but there wasn't one teacher in evidence in the center part, where all the activity was going on. "The kids ran it. They ran it, they carried it off, they knew what to do. One team organized the whole thing, but every team contributed, so that it was a whole school thing."

Jason Caine — Future Mayor of Attleboro

Jason Caine, an eighth-grade student who is one of Dave Cox's team members, was in charge of invited guests, along with his committee partner, Alison Frenier. They made up the list of proposed guests (which included the city council) and checked it with Cox's co-teacher. Then Jason called each guest on the phone, and left his home phone number for those who were out when he called, so they could call him back.

"He complained when he came back from vacation, 'You know, I couldn't go anywhere over vacation; I had all those calls coming into my house; I had to be there to take them!' " Forbes said. "And when all these important people came to the school, did they ask for the principal? Did they ask for the teacher? No, they asked for Jason! They wanted Jason.

"What I guess I'm seeing is the factor of kids taking on responsibility for the school; for instance, David's kids do our courtyard. We had a huge committee service day here last year; we redid the courtyard and the landscaping, and our kids keep it up. They deal with trash, they dig up weeds, they do all kinds of things out there."

Robert J. Coelho Middle School

75 Brown Street
Attleboro, Massachusetts 02703

Phone: 508-761-7551
FAX: 508-399-6506

Looping grades: 5-6, 7-8

Open to visitors: yes

Contact: Mimi Forbes, Principal
Dave Cox, Teacher

Community Service

Once a month, said Cox, "I stuff my home room onto a
bus and take them across town to Operation Headstart."
There the students are assigned to a particular classroom—
about five eighth-grade students to each room, the same
room each time, to help out the children, "the little tykes,
about four or five years old," Cox said. [Miss Puccio's home
room goes two weeks later.] The eighth graders stay for an
hour and a half each visit, and don't want to leave.

"They're getting to know the kids really well, and they're
beginning to realize, they're God to these little kids! And it's
a beautiful thing for them; it does a great, great thing for
them."

The class was recently invited for bagels and coffee for
"Volunteer Appreciation Day" in Attleboro to thank them
for their volunteer work with the Headstart kids.

"It's No Accident"

Dave Cox calls his students "nice kids — a great group of
kids." He goes on to say, "It's not an accident. We work hard
at it."

He sees his partner, Pam Puccio, as a good match for him.
"Pam and I have the same basic ideas on how to deal with
kids. For instance, she doesn't start the class by yelling at
the kids. I don't think I've ever heard her yell. It's the same
with me; we don't do those things. We just start the class,
and try to have a pretty good time while we're at it."

Block Scheduling Provides (Some) Flexibility

Cox and his partner tend to schedule big blocks of time
for their instruction; Cox does a lot of hands-on activities
with his students, particularly in science. But he wishes he
had more time. "Doing what we're doing takes a lot of
time," he said. He and Puccio schedule on a day-to-day
basis; if one person is working on something that takes two
to four hours of time, they will adjust the schedule. They
also combine their classes for many joint projects.

Their seventh-grade experience was more flexible than
eighth grade, because of the eighth-grade requirement of
first-period Algebra I. "And then you almost have to have
another math class during the day, for all the other kids
from the three teams. So that drives your math; and it
messes up the day for our first and second mods [modules],
as far as we're concerned." Cox would prefer to handle
math within the team, to retain the flexibility in scheduling
that he had in seventh grade, and defer formalized Algebra
I to ninth grade.

Cox spreads his instructional content over a two-year
period. "In grade seven we're supposed to be doing mostly

life science, and in grade eight physics, which is a blend of astronomy, chemistry and physics. I can do the material out of order; so I can study the stars in grade seven, or in grade eight, or both — which I've tried to do, actually. When I do density, specific gravity, things like that, I introduce it in the seventh grade, and then do it again in the eighth in a bit more complicated way."

In one hour-and-fifteen-minute-long session, Cox covered rocks. "I like rocks," he said. He used material both from a grade-five level Golden Book and an adult level book to teach a multilevel class on metamorphic, sedimentary, igneous and conglomerate rocks. "I haven't used the text-book yet, and I have no intention of doing so," Cox said. The students spent the class categorizing various rocks.

Because of the two-year arrangement, Cox knows what his eighth grade students have covered the previous year.

"In the past, when I reminded kids what they were sup-posed to have covered, normally the kids would say, 'The teacher never taught us anything.' Now I can say, 'Well, I remember teaching this myself, actually.' And I've saved a lot of their papers from the previous year, so I can go get them and hold them up, and say, 'Remember the paper we did? See how you're supposed to know that?' It's kind of interesting like that."

Connecting the Curriculum and the Community

Cox likes to integrate his curriculum with resources and events in the community; to do so, he involves both guest speakers coming into class and bus trips to various places in Attleboro.

He — and his students — grab every opportunity they can in this regard. After the Earth Day celebration, one of his students, Jason Caine, came across some workers from the new municipal water and sewage treatment plant at the middle school. "He came running up to me and said, 'How would you like a guest speaker?' I said, 'Sure,' so he said, 'I'll go ask Miss Puccio,' and off he went. So we rolled those guys in, they had all their equipment and everything, and we had guest speakers for half an hour — which was really neat, because they had just put a 26 million dollar water treatment plant in Attleboro that went on line last June."

Cox had Xeroxed the story out of the paper and taught a unit on the plant at that time, so he and the students were very familiar with how the plant operated. "So when the workers said, 'Oh, would you guys like to come to the plant?' I said 'Yeah, sure.' So he gave me his card, and said, 'Just call.' Jason took the card and said, 'I'll take care of that.' "

of a two-year in fifth and sixth grade because it wasn't working out; it helped a lot. I liked my second year. In sixth grade it was really great, but I did have that happen to me."

John pointed out that's why the class has teambuilding activities, so "we can get more comfortable with the teacher if we don't really like her that much."

Brian felt that there should be a period of time at the beginning of the first year where students could give a teacher feedback on how they think the teacher is doing. "If a student has a real problem with a teacher he should be able to change teams," Brian said. "There should be some time at the beginning of the year when you can change.

"In fifth and sixth grade I wasn't being challenged enough; there wasn't enough for me to do; and basically most of the time we just — sat there."

Dave Cox asked the students, "What if you had a teacher that you really couldn't stand?" Paulina re-sponded, "Bad deal!" John told about his experience in fifth and sixth grade; he didn't participate in class, and ended up getting C+ on everything; about his teacher, he said, "I say that she hated me." Apparently John did manage to mend some fences with the teacher after he left her class; "I think she does, now she does [like him]; I talk to her in the hallway all the time, and she says, 'I'm glad I can talk to you now.' I was in her class with my committee last term; I was tutoring in her class." Cox asked, "How did that work out?" John said, "Okay. I was there when the other teacher was in class."

Math Class: Math class was a sticking point for the students, partly because they felt the teacher didn't know them

Continued on page 100

Continued from page 99

as well as the students on her own team, and partly because they were used to more input and discussion than they were allowed in her class. Teacher style entered into it also, and the students were vocal about expressing what they felt were her shortcomings.

Jason said, "I kind of respect our own teacher [Miss Puccio] more, because we'd go over the homework, and then she'd give us a quiz, then the next time go over the homework—. This teacher only takes five minutes, and we have to write down three pages of notes, and then we're off to the next assignment. We can't even talk to her about the lesson, because we don't have time. We always have to do a test or something."

Paulina chimed in. "Yeah, and the quizzes are like four questions, so each question is worth 25 points; so it's kind of hard." Paulina did admit that, since the students were used to Dave Cox and Pam Puccio, who let them take on a lot of responsibility, that they might be judging teachers with a different teaching style harder.

Brian added, "I think she just doesn't respect kids from other teams as much as she respects kids from her team, because she doesn't know our capabilities."

The Expectations Team has picked up a couple students from other teams, "unhappy campers," according to Cox, who just weren't working out where they were. One student was moved into Cox's team at the beginning of the seventh grade, "so he's happy." The team hasn't lost anyone due to incompatibility.

All past experiences aside, the students are obviously thriving on the Expectations Team. They have an easy relationship with Cox, where a mix of comraderie and respect flow back and forth between them; they feel free to express themselves honestly about their concerns and their ideas. And one other thing is evident about how they feel about Mr. Cox: they love the guy.

You Take A Bus—

One thing Cox likes about the small, 50-student team, is that "you can stuff 'em all on one bus. You don't have to worry about being split up, or going with another team that you don't know, or having two buses and only one teacher on the bus. We're all there, we're together, we get on and go."

Cox has bussed his team to the local newspaper, to a radio station, and to the fire station. "The fire station was fabulous," Cox said. The chief is a great guy. He knew we were coming, and when he found out it was us, he called in guys from other stations — guys that had certain skills. He called in Mr. Goyette, one of my former students, to do a demonstration on the airpack; they had the guys demo the EMT stuff; they really pulled all the stops for us. And then of course we invited all those people to the team breakfast, so that they could come and get a free meal out of it."

The students can catch the municipal bus right outside their school. "They charge us half-price, because we're a school group, so for 35 cents the kids can get a tour of the water treatment plant. And the small team — 49, 50 kids — helps. You just couldn't do this with 125 kids. Just the planning would drive you crazy. With the 50 kids, you stuff 'em on the one bus, you go.

"It's a beautiful thing."

CHAPTER 7

Class Dynamics
A Powerful Factor in Multiyear Classes

The fourth-grade team at A. Irvin Studley Elementary School takes a different approach than the two- and three-person teams at other Attleboro schools. The teachers on this team teach alone in their self-contained classrooms, and meet once a week with their principal, Dolores Fitzgerald, to discuss common concerns.

Taking part in the discussion were principal Fitzgerald, fourth-grade teachers Cindy Edwards, Phyllis Sisson, and Lisa Hopkins, third-grade teacher Connie O'Riley, and student teacher Kim Tobin. Assistant Superintendent Ted Thibodeau was also present.

The teachers at the fourth grade team meeting spoke about the multiyear assignment with the air of veterans; all are in either the first or second year of their second assignment, which gives them a certain perspective on the practice. All had very positive things to say; they also all voiced some concerns, which centered primarily on class dynamics.

"As far as how much the children have learned and the difference between having a class for one year as opposed to having them for two years," Lisa Hopkins said, "there's an incredible difference. There's none of that getting to know you phase in the beginning of the year; you hit the ground running and you don't stop. You know what they've been taught because you've had them the previous year, and can build on that. I've seen — and it's happened two times, so it must be the case — that we've gotten so much further than I have with just having the class for one year."

New Kids Fit Right In

The teachers have had mostly positive experiences with new students fitting in easily with the rest of the group. Lisa Hopkins got two new students this year, "and they've just slid right in, like they've been here all the time." Connie O'Riley, a third-grade teacher sitting in on the session, also reported a positive experience upon receiving five new students in her fourth grade class the previous year.

"I was amazed at how well they fit right in; everyone else was very supportive and pitched right in; it was all one big happy family. It was a neat group." She did report having to do some teambuilding. "Because some of the kids were so new, every so often we'd be talking, and then I'd realize, my God, these kids don't know what we're talking about; the kids who've been here for two years are so tight." O'Riley uses a lot of two-year themes in her class; the veterans of the class had to in and fill the new children in. "They've helped out tremendously, which is a great opportunity for them, also."

Phyllis Sisson had a bigger challenge in integrating her class. She taught second grade one year, then moved up to third grade with her class. There was a fairly large influx of new students in the third grade; then she went to fourth grade, and some of the children left to go on to another class. With the large number of new students in the third grade, it was almost as if there were two separate groups of children. She feels it was tough on the new kids.

"The family that builds [in a multiyear classroom] is very tight; we had to do a lot of teambuilding to help the new children feel comfortable," Sisson said.

Parent Support

Sisson also reported some "wonderful parent support; much more so than when I had them for one year." She described the comfort level as "fantastic," in terms of volunteering time, or finding out what the class needed. "I've always had good luck with my parents," Sisson said, "but now it's more like having a friend. It's also a big school, and having the same parents for two years makes it easier to think of the school as more of a neighborhood school, because you get to know the families that much more."

She feels she's made breakthroughs with parents that she may not have been able to reach without the two-year relationship, and the few times she hasn't been able to reach a parent, "At least I know I've tried. I'm not knocking my head against the wall." The two-year assignment actually seems to have given her more of a perspective on the few parents who haven't come through.

Some Complications

All three fourth-grade teachers reported wonderful experiences with one of their two-year assignments—and problems with the others. The problems centered on the dynamics of the class, especially the interrelationships among a few of the students.

"For the particular group I have now, dynamically it's wonderful," said Cindy Edwards, "but the last group I had, the children were really tired of each other by the end of two years. It was especially true of my girls; I had some very strong, very social girls, who were dealing with a lot of the kinds of issues that usually come up in middle school."

"I'm having that trouble now," Phyllis Sisson said. "My first session was great; I would have been happy to follow them right along; but with this group, at this point they don't even like each other. It's difficult to put them into teams, because nobody wants to sit with this one—again, it's a group of strong-willed girls. They do make life miserable for a lot of the kids, and they're really sick of each other. I didn't notice that with my first group; it depends on the mix."

Lisa Hopkins noticed some problems in her first year of her second group. "My first time doing this I had a wonderful group, and I was raring to go. Then last year I had two boys that really made a big difference. They were really serious behavior problems. The dynamics of the class were unbelievable. They're both gone; one moved, and the other was transferred to another class and then left and went to a private school. It's like a completely different class this year; the whole dynamics have changed."

"You have to focus in on the class dynamics and the people in the room," Phyllis Sisson said. "It's hard to get this particular group to work together.

"The first group I had was great! They worked together, they liked each other, they were always willing to work on teams — but I can't do it now.

"At this point I think I'm getting tired of the behaviors that I've dealt with for two years. At this point, you just want to say, 'Snap out of it.' "

The members of the fourth grade team seemed to agree that students who "just couldn't seem to get along" needed another option, like having them move to a different teacher each year.

A Different Perspective

Principal Dolores Fitzgerald said that she'd had the girls in question in her office and asked them about the situation, and as she said, " They're not unhappy with the arrangement; they're pleased with their classroom."

Attleboro does review each student's placement at the end of every year, and does move individual students if it seems to be in the best interests of the student; or in the instance of a parent's request. There is no procedure in place for dealing with an entire class that seems to be dysfunctional.

Asked how he would handle the situation, Assistant Superintendent Thibodeau indicated that, rather than move students or break up a class, he would like to see teachers having such difficulties teamed with teachers who are strong in team-building and in dealing with the kinds of social issues arising in the classes.

A. Irvin Studley Elementary School

299 Rathbun Willard Drive
Attleboro, Massachusetts 02703

Phone: 508-222-2621
FAX: 508-226-0419

Looping grades: 1-2, 3-4

Open to visitors: Yes

Contact: Dolores Fitzgerald, principal

Look Before You Loop

L ooping is a simple concept, and it's much easier to implement than many of the reforms teachers struggle to incorporate into their classrooms. There is also very little that can go wrong.

However, both teachers and parents express a few very legitimate concerns about the multiyear teacher-student arrangement. Fortunately, all of these concerns can be addressed and resolved.

The Marginal Teacher

Probably the biggest concern parents have when considering a multiyear arrangement for their child is, "What if my child gets a bad teacher for two years?"

Schools following conventional curriculum guidelines tend to introduce new concepts and content in grades one, three, five and seven, and to review and reinforce the concepts and content in grades two, four, six and eight. This sort of "introduction and review" cycle actually acts as a buffer between students and a poorly performing teacher; an academically solid student can usually survive a year with a poor teacher because he or she will be exposed to the content for two years in a row. It's not the best arrangement in the world, and arguably a poor teacher shouldn't be teaching for one year, let alone two; but the reality is that it's almost impossible for a school system to unseat a tenured teacher.

However, the stakes go up dramatically in terms of teacher performance when the multiyear configuration is introduced. Even the best student will be impacted heavily by two years with a poorly performing teacher; kids who need more attention and guidance from a classroom teacher simply won't survive academically.

The good news is that marginal teachers don't generally volunteer for new or innovative programs; it's too much work. The onus is on the school's administration: where a principal or superintendent has the choice of assigning a teacher to a single-year or multiyear classroom, he or she must protect the students from poor teachers and assign only willing and capable teachers to the multiyear classrooms.

For one school's criteria when hiring teachers for their multiyear teaching assignments, see pages 31–32.

A Teacher/Student Personality Clash

Another concern, brought up more by parents than by teachers, is the possibility of a personality conflict between a teacher and a particular student. "That teacher just hates my kid!" is an occasional complaint among parents. Many times it's due to a misunderstanding that can be resolved; sometimes it's true.

Before You Transfer a Student — Some Steps You Can Take to Resolve a Teacher-Student Conflict

by Yvette Zgonc

With any student, it's important to establish a code of conduct with guidelines or rules of behavior, and to make it clear that students understand how these guidelines fit into every situation: in learning centers, in small groups, outside the classroom in the cafeteria and hallway, and so forth. In a multiyear situation, which is conducive to working cooperatively in small groups, it's also necessary to make it clear how the guidelines translate to small group activities.

When a Personality Clash Arises

When a teacher finds herself or himself locked in a personality conflict with a student, there are a number of strategies that can be tried before deciding to transfer the student.

1. First, ask yourself what you can do to help this kid succeed in class. Have you tried everything you can think of?
2. One of the best strategies is to conference with the kid, to talk about the problems he or she is having.
3. Talk to other colleagues who have had the child; what has worked for them?
4. Bring in the parents. Use the services of a guidance counselor, if possible, to help mediate the discussion.

If you've given it your best shot, and the issues between you and the child have not improved, you can then can discuss transferring the child to another classroom.

I am careful not to give the message to the child that, if there's a personality conflict, the child may be transferred to a different class; the child may get the idea that, "If I'm really bad, I can get out of this class."

The Multiyear Classroom as a Place to Resolve Issues

First, it should be accepted that the two-year classroom is tailor-made for difficult students. The shy child, the special-needs child, the emotionally fragile child — even the "bully" of the class — need the stability and security of a long-term relationship and a predictable environment, probably more than the more resilient kids in the class. The supportive structure of the class actually gives teachers, parents, and support staff more time to introduce appropriate interventions for these children and work toward resolving some of the difficulties that are hindering their growth. Yvette Zgonc, a nationally-known lecturer on cooperative discipline, says,

> The multiyear situation can be very positive, especially for difficult children, who don't do well with change; the connection with a teacher can enhance their self-esteem, and make them feel comfortable.

The most important thing, says, Zgonc, is to try to provide students with a sense of belonging. All children, especially difficult children, need to feel that they're making a contribution to the class.

"One way to do this is to have kids helping kids," Zgonc says. Pairing a difficult child with another student who needs tutoring is a great way to bolster the child's self-esteem.

On the negative side, kids don't always show the kind of results that teachers might hope for, even with a dedicated teacher trying every strategy and intervention she or he can think of. Sometimes the positive results of work with a teacher don't show up until years afterward.

"I have seen some really good teachers try everything they could think of, and don't see any positive results, and they get really frustrated," says Zgonc.

Zgonc has some recommendations for teachers facing a conflict with a difficult student (see *Before you Transfer a Student*, this page). Esther Wright, author of *Loving Discipline A to Z* and *Good Morning Class — I Love You!* also has some advice on defining the needs of difficult children (see *"What Does This Student Need?"* on page 108).

It's important for teachers to realize that, as human beings, it's not possible for them to like every student; and that there are times when, for a particular student's best interest, a transfer to another classroom is the best solution.

The best way to avoid a long-term mismatch between teacher and student in a multiyear class is for the teacher and administration, as a matter of policy, to review each student's placement with the student and parents at the end of every school year, and decide whether to continue or change the class assignment for that student. The parents (and teachers) should also have the option to request a student's transfer mid-year if necessary.

Too Many High-Impact Kids

Teaching today is vastly different than it was just twenty years ago. Today's teachers are faced with a student population that comes to school with a wide variety of complex problems. Many children enter school with health problems and developmental delays because of:

- low birth weight
- premature or traumatic birth
- untreated health problems
- exposure to toxic substances, like lead paint
- lack of prenatal care
- drug damage at birth

Additionally, the schools are dealing with children who are homeless, or from families in crisis; they may have attended an inadequate day care program; they may not have been exposed to preschool at all. They may be emotionally or physically neglected or abused; they may be showing signs of stress because of a harried family existence.

Then there are physically disabled children, slow learners, and learning-disabled children who require a variety of special services in addition to regular classroom teaching.

Some problems are a byproduct of poverty; others are a symptom of an increasingly fragmented, fast-paced society. As a result we have a greater number of children in school today who impact greatly on instruction.

Because the multiyear classroom is such a supportive environment for high-needs children, there may be a tendency among some administrators to assign too many of them to a multiyear program. This can overwhelm the teacher and create parental opposition, as parents perceive their child's class as turning into a "special ed" class.

Each teacher's capacity for dealing with high-needs children is different; some teachers have very "broad shoulders," while others are quickly overwhelmed by a lot of high-maintenance kids. However, even the teacher with the reputation for broad shoulders may find herself overwhelmed as her principal asks her to take "just one more special kid." Here are some general guidelines to consider when placing high-impact children in a multiyear setting.

1. Include the same percentage of high-needs children in the multiyear class as in a single-year class.

This is not a good message; a better message is that the child may not like his or her teacher all the time, but can learn ways to deal with the situation and succeed.

In my experience most transfers are requested by parents, rather than by teachers. Most teachers do everything they can to try to work it out with students in spite of difficulties. Some parents, on the other hand, are very quick to demand transfer for their children, and some schools end up playing "musical chairs" with their students. I myself believe in a very cautious approach in changing a student's placement.

It's impossible for every human being to like every other human being; I tell teachers it's all right not to like your kids — as long as your feeling is not telegraphed to the child.

My advice is to act as if the child walks into the classroom every day with the label, "I am a responsible, caring human being." If a child comes into the classroom every day with the negative label that you've assigned, it's going to be very difficult to overcome that and help the child succeed.

If, in spite of every intervention and strategy that you and the child's parents devise, the situation does not improve, and you see the child's self-esteem dwindling, then it's time to consider another placement for the child.

Yvette Zgonc lectures nationwide on the topics of discipline, special needs and ADD/ADHD in the classroom. She is a contributor to the revised edition of Cooperative Discipline, *by Linda Albert, and is currently at work on a book of her own on the topic of developmental discipline.*

WHAT DOES THIS STUDENT NEED?

This is the most important question to ask when dealing with chronic, persistent misbehavior. Use the following list as a menu, remembering that different students respond to different interventions based on their needs and the causes of their behaviors.

Does this student need . . .

❑ More success and validation?

❑ Opportunities to be a leader and contribute?

❑ More specific or clearer guidelines for behavior?

❑ A behavior management contract?

❑ A mentor or buddy?

❑ An opportunity to communicate? *(journal writing, drawing, counseling)*

❑ An opportunity to "let off steam"? *(jogging, punching clay, kicking balls)*

❑ More rigorous consequences *(only after natural and logical ones have failed)*

❑ Good role models?

❑ More one-to-one attention? *(aides, volunteers, peer tutors)*

❑ Shorter assignments? *(for students with short attention spans or cognitive delays)*

❑ More choice regarding assignments and classroom activities?

❑ Parental support?

❑ More tangible rewards?

❑ A special quiet place?

❑ Conflict resolution skills training?

From Loving Discipline A to Z, *by Esther Wright. ©1995, Esther Wright.*

2. Make sure the teacher has a voice in defining the needs of each student.
3. Reserve teachers the right to request a child be placed in another class. A procedure for this should be developed and presented to parents at the outset of the multiyear program.
4. Reduce class size for teachers who choose to take more than their share of high-needs children.
5. Provide training and classroom support as needed for teachers expected to deal with high-needs children.
6. Allow teachers the deciding vote when deciding second-year placement in the multiyear classroom.

The Class From Hell

The Herdmans were absolutely the worst kids in the history of the world. They lied and stole and smoked cigars (even the girls) and talked dirty and hit little kids and cussed their teachers and took the name of the Lord in vain and set fire to Fred Shoemaker's old broken-down toolhouse.

from The Best Christmas Pageant Ever, by Barbara Robinson

Every so often a class comes along that seems to be totally dysfunctional. Whether there are too many summer-born boys, or too many dominant personalities, or whether there was an alignment of the outer planets when this particular class was born, some classes just never seem to gel. One teacher described her worst class like this:

As a group the whole class was disjointed. There were too many students with difficult behavior problems clumped together in one group. The class was top-heavy with special-needs students, and to top it off this year was my largest class to date. To make matters worse, this class had very little parental support.

Teaching in such a classroom environment is stressful and discouraging to most teachers. A classroom of needy students is very demanding on a teacher's time and energy, and a classroom like the one described above may be too much for even a veteran teacher.

This type of high-needs class may require a variety of services to augment the efforts of the classroom teacher: special education intervention, Title I support, and perhaps pull-out programs for some students and full inclusion for others. High-needs students often need remediation in several areas at once.

Road-Testing the Class

One approach in safeguarding against a dysfunctional class is to road-test the class; that is, to defer making a final commitment to looping until getting a good understanding of the dynamics of that particular group of students.

By November, a class should be operating smoothly, for the most part. Your students should understand the class rules and guidelines and be well on their way to becoming a close-knit, supportive group of children. If it's evident that there are problems, some analysis is in order. Ask yourself these questions:

- Have I tried child-centered discipline strategies?
- Have I introduced acceptance activities to help children understand diversity and special needs?
- Have I set up clear, understandable guidelines for the children in the class? Better yet, have I given the children input into setting up the class guidelines or rules?
- Is the entire class dysfunctional, or are there a few students creating most of the problems? (See page 110 for "Turning Around the 'Down.' ")
- Can I introduce conflict resolution strategies to help quarreling children resolve their difficulties?

One Man's Herdsman . . .

If you and the administration have determined that you do have a dysfunctional class, you have several alternatives:

1. You may be able to transfer a few students at the end of the first year and loop with the rest of the class. (In some instances, you may want to consider transferring students now.)
2. You may want to break up the class at the end of the year, redistributing the students to several other teachers, and start over with a new class next year.
3. There may be a teacher who is more attuned to handling this particular class of individuals, and who is willing to take it on for the coming year. (What one teacher may consider dysfunctional, another may consider dynamic.) Make sure this teacher understands what he or she is getting into.

Whatever you do, don't dump the entire class on your unsuspecting would-be looping partner. Without the consent of an informed teacher and lots of intervention strategies, you're just condemning your partner to the same bumpy ride.

If the administration has agreed to the road-test approach prior to the beginning of the school year, it should stick to its promise and allow the two teachers involved in the looping arrangement to make the final decision about whether or not to loop with this particular class.

Parental Support for This Approach

It's important to inform the parents of this approach before beginning the first year, and make sure they understand and support you. Once you have decided not to loop with this particular class, notify the parents immediately. You will probably find that many of the parents already have concerns about their children's class.

A Caveat

You've analyzed the class; you've decided it's dysfunctional; you have agreed with the administration to break up the class and stay at the same grade level next year. You've contacted the parents, and they agree with you that it would be better not to keep this particular class together.

Now you tell the kids.

"But you did this with the last class!" "My sister Jennie's class is looping!" "So is my brother Joe's!" "But every kid in school is looping!"

"You hate us!"

Breaking up a class is serious business. If children have already been introduced to the concept of looping, and especially if they have expectations because other classes have already experienced looping, they are bound to take your decision to heart. Some children may understand, and may be relieved — a truly dysfunctional class adds stress to the children's lives, as well as the teacher's — but there are also going to be hurt feelings.

It is therefore important to try every alternative before deciding to disband a class, and when the decision is reached, it's important to be as honest as you possibly can about the decision. If you lie to them, they will know.

Turning Around the "Down"
by Irv Richardson

Sooner or later it happens to everyone who teaches a classroom full of young people. You realize that things in the classroom aren't what you know they should be . . . kids are squabbling with each other, the assigned work isn't getting done, your energy isn't spent on teaching but instead on putting out the small brush fires combusting all over the classroom. The class has entered a negative cycle that needs an immediate "direction correction."

When I found my class headed into a negative spiral, quick action on my part was the first and most important step in turning the situation around. By following certain steps I was able to act like the cowboy who jumps on the back of the horses of the runaway stagecoach and slowly brings back order and direction back to the classroom. You can use the same steps:

STEP ONE: Realize that the class is comprised of individuals.

The way to turn the class around is to think about each individual member of the class. I found it effective to go through the class list and decide whether each individual student was making positive or negative contributions to the class. If I felt a student was making positive contributions, I would put a "+" next to the student's name. If I felt the student wasn't making positive contributions or being a productive member of the class, I would put a "–" next to that name.

After proceeding through the entire class list, I would go back and note the individuals I felt were not making positive contributions. Almost always, I found that there were many more "plusses" than "minuses." It wasn't the entire class that wasn't being productive; it was usually just a few individuals who were giving me my negative impression of the class.

STEP TWO: Realize that to change the behavior of the students, you must first change the behavior of the most important person in the class — you.

If the tone and the classroom climate are going to change, it is up to the teacher to initiate the change. Changing your behavior means that you have to pay greater attention to the things that are going well, and then decide upon specific steps you can take to help the students who aren't making good use of their time in class.

Go back to your class list. For each student whose name has a plus, write down one or two specific things the student is doing that you want to recognize as helping the class. It might be that he is getting his work done well or is helping keep the classroom neat or organized. Perhaps she is showing problem-solving or leadership skills.

For the students with a "–" after their names, think about the one behavior or action that you feel is most disruptive to the class. Perhaps someone is physically hurting classmates or not finishing classwork. List the specific behavior that you want to eliminate.

STEP THREE: Now that you've listed both positive and negative student behaviors, you need to develop specific plans to recognize positive behaviors and to work at changing the negative behaviors.

A good method is to divide your plan into two parts:

 1. What you plan to do for each individual student; and
 2. How you plan to share both your praise and concerns with the class.

Write a personal note to the children you feel are contributing to the class, expressing your appreciation and thanking them. (An alternative is to write the letter to the children's parents.) This will not only give the children recognition for their contributions, it will also reinforce your belief that there are indeed positive things happening in your classroom.

You can also make a list of the positive behaviors on a chart (without listing the names of specific individuals) and display that in the classroom.

For students whose behavior needs to change, develop specific steps to help each student change his or her behavior. For example, if you have a student who constantly interrupts you, you need to discuss his behavior with him privately, and explain that the behavior interferes with the other students' ability to learn. Let him know that you will be keeping track of the interruptions, and that you and he will work together to change his behavior.

Develop a plan that involves reasonable, related and respectful consequences for the student's disruptive behavior, and provide alternative ways for the student to act when confronted with situations that tend to initiate this type of behavior.

You can also list the unacceptable classroom behaviors on a chart and display it (without listing the culprits.) Discuss the list and the reasons that these behaviors are not good for the class.

Communicate with the students' parents, either in a note or by phone, explaining your concerns about their children's behavior, and explaining the steps you plan to take to help their children develop more positive behaviors.

STEP FOUR: Let your class know that your own behavior is going to change — and why.

The first time I used this process, I came into the classroom ready to change things and didn't inform the students that I was going to be using a different approach toward some classroom behaviors. This created a lot of tension when the students became aware that I was acting differently toward them.

It's better to explain to the class why you came to the decision to change things — there are some things happening in class that make it difficult for the class to run smoothly, etc. — and what you plan to do to alter the negative behaviors and reinforce positive behaviors. Discuss the lists you've made, get the students' input, and make them a part of the process.

STEP FIVE: Hold class meetings.

Class meetings are an excellent way to involve the students in the smooth functioning of the class. In my classroom we held class meetings on a regular basis, using the class meeting format suggested by Jane Nelsen in her book, *Positive Discipline*. As Dr. Nelson suggests in her book, we held our class meetings for four reasons:

1. to give compliments
2. to help each other
3. to solve problems
4. to plan events

I used one of these regularly scheduled class meetings to bring up my concerns about how things were going in our classroom. I shared the positive behaviors (without student names) that I thought were helping us as a class; then I shared the unhelpful behaviors (again, without the names of the responsible students), that I felt were not making positive contributions to our class. Often, this list would bring snickers along with some furtive glances, as students identified those responsible for the behavior.

I used the meeting to let the class know I would be sending home notes to parents, and that these notes would share the positive things happening in the class, as well as ask for the parents' help in solving some of the problems individual students were having.

We also used the meeting to solicit student opinions about how they felt the class was going and what things they felt were, and were not, going well. As a class, we listed the things we could do to help make the class go more smoothly.

I also let the students know that I would be meeting soon with some individuals in the class to talk about specific plans that I had to help those individuals.

STEP SIX: Follow through.

Once you've analyzed the situation, developed plans, and discussed those plans with the class, you need to follow through. By following through with your plans on a consistent basis, you will emphasize the importance of your students' ability to work as a group, as well as your confidence in their ability to change. A byproduct of this is that you will discover, as I did, that your own confidence in your ability as "class manager," capable of positively affecting the classroom environment, will grow.

Continued Parent-Teacher Conflict

The multiyear program tends to foster strong, positive and supportive relationships between teachers and parents. However, every teacher has dealt with parents who are unreasonable or downright hostile.

Some parents may not support the multiyear concept itself; others may disagree with your teaching methods, or have unrealistic expectations for their child. Whatever the reason, it's painful for a teacher to deal with belligerent and demanding parents for a single year, never mind two.

Perhaps the most important question is, how is this conflict affecting the child? The multiyear relationship is so valuable to children, that if the child in question is having a positive experience in your class, and if you can keep the battle between you and the parents and not get the child caught in the middle, you should do *everything in your power* to salvage, or at least tolerate, the relationship.

The first thing to determine is, what are the parents' issues? Are there misconceptions about how the class is operating, or how assessment is being performed, that a good discussion might solve? Are there issues of a personal nature — a perceived slight of either the parents or the child — that can be resolved?

Also, be aware that complaints voiced by parents may reflect deeper, unarticulated issues. Class and cultural differences may also enter into misunderstandings between teacher and parents. You may have to be a bit of a detective to find out the real issues bothering parents.

Mediation involving the principal and/or the counseling staff may help. Be sure to bring any in specialists or support staff involved in the issue to help the discussion.

If it's obvious that the disagreement is impacting negatively on the child, or if the situation is unresolvable and intolerable, then you may have to consider transferring the child to another class. This is where a built-in, standard year-end evaluation process for each child's placement is valuable; if parents are that adamantly opposed to you and your methods, they will probably leap at the chance to move their child to another class.

Hidden Disabilities

One of the benefits of multiyear programs is that they reduce the need for special-needs placements (Rappa, 1993, see page 15). Sometimes all a child needs is a little extra learning time and a stable, supportive classroom environment to catch on to learning. Part of the reason for the reduction may be that children who do need a little extra learning time are mistakenly (or deliberately) identified as special-needs in order to get special help.

However, there will be children in the looping classroom who need more than a little extra time; they have learning disabilities that are not necessarily obvious, and that will require special services. The fact that a multiyear teacher is able to delay a high-stakes decision like retention should not prevent him or her from doing the kind of ongoing assessment and evaluation of students that would catch a potential learning disability.

The Halo Effect

The multiyear teacher most often gets to know his or her students extremely well, both academically and personally, and has a depth of understanding of how the child learns, his or her strengths and weaknesses, and any special needs he or she may have.

However, the strong bonding that takes place between teacher and child in a multiyear relationship can sometimes create an atmosphere where a teacher is more "forgiving" of her student's academic shortcomings. This "halo effect" can get in the way of some teachers seeing potential learning problems, and can have potentially serious problems for the student if necessary special needs intervention is delayed.

Too Attached to Leave?

One concern some parents express when considering looping is that their child will become too attached to his or her teacher, and that it will be even more painful to leave after two years.

Teachers and parents report some very emotional separations at the end of the two-year program. It *is* hard, on the children and on the teachers; and with children who find transitions or separation very difficult, it can be doubly hard.

The question is, Do we avoid developing deep relationships because someday we will have to say goodbye?

One Rhode Island teacher reported that she had a boy who had a very hard time with transitions; she and the boy's parents were very worried once it came time for him to leave his two-year classroom and move on. It turned out the boy was looking forward to the change, and to making new friends. Apparently the two years with this teacher and this class had given him an emotional foundation that made him ready to step out into the world.

Most looping programs that have been in existence for awhile have found the need to develop strategies for aiding the students' transition to their next classroom experience—visits to the new classrooms and their teachers, interviews with students who have already made the transition, some whole-school projects that allow students from different classes to visit and make friends. All of these help to ease transitions. Teacher Char Forsten advises,

> Many times, not only are the children leaving their teacher, but the group itself is breaking up, which can be traumatic. It's important to help children transition to their next class.
>
> It's especially important to do a lot of preparation for the next situation, in a positive, realistic way. Let them know what to expect in their new surroundings. (Don't tell them how much more homework they're going to have, or how much they're going to miss you.)
>
> Some kids are ready to go on and make new friends, and others have a tough time. Prepare them for the move. Take them to the next place; also have kids come in from the new place and

provide a question and answer period for the students. Make sure you bring in kids who adapted easily, as well as some who had a tough time.

Also, make sure that the students know they can come back and visit. One class at Cyril K. Brennan Middle School in Attleboro, Massachusetts, actually had a reunion a few weeks into the new year. (See "*Kindred Spirits,*" page 91.)

The bonds that are forged in a long-term teacher-student relationship are not easily broken, even with separation. Many teachers report a deep and strong connection with their students, years after their time together in school.

SOME HIDDEN CONSEQUENCES

Moving to another grade level can have unforeseen consequences that impact dramatically on the teacher. The following possibilities need to be considered:

A teacher who changes grade levels may suddenly find herself without a teaching assistant. Most of the paid, full-time teaching assistants work in kindergarten and first grade. A teacher wanting to move with her class from first to second grade will have the same students, with the same needs, but will probably find that her teaching assistant has "stayed back," having been assigned to first grade. While it makes sense for a teaching assistant to move, with her class and its teacher, to the next grade level, it is not a reality in the vast majority of today's school systems. Some teachers have actually decided against looping, preferring instead to keep their teaching assistant.

A teacher must master the curriculum of his new grade. This is good; increased knowledge helps a teacher teach his students, and furthers career development. However, it involves a commitment of time on the part of the teacher, and (one would hope) money for staff development on the part of the school district.

A teacher may need special training for grade-specific curriculum requirements at the next grade level. Health units are very often grade-specific, and require specific training. DARE, a drug-program administered and taught by local police departments around the country, is also very grade-specific and requires special training for classroom teachers.

In some states, a teacher may need an additional certification to teach at the next grade level. Florida, for instance, requires a K-1 teacher to be certified for both grades. Teachers and administrators need to check with their state's department of education before deciding to loop.

A teacher needs to learn about the ages and stages of the students at both grade levels. Children's developmental needs and behavior patterns change dramatically from one year to the next, and strategies that are successful at one stage may not work for the next. (The book *Yardsticks*, by Chip Wood, provides a good overview of developmental stages.)

A teacher may find that her new grade level has state- or locally-mandated testing, curriculum content, and/or promotional standards. Standardized testing, most often mandated at grades three or four, can add tremendously to the pressure a teacher feels. Specific curriculum content may require additional training on the part of the teacher, and specific promotional standards not only restrict a teacher's decision-making power in regards to her students' progress, they could possibly torpedo a looping teacher's desire to give certain students more learning time should she decide to loop for a third year.

A looping teacher may find himself with a case of separation anxiety, if the set-up of the school requires him to move his class to a different wing. Long-established friendships with colleagues, as well as some teaming relationships, may be disrupted with the move.

A teacher may find herself in a grade level that is not child-centered philosophically. Kindergarten, first, and second grades are generally very experiential in nature. Teachers and children sing, chant, paint, dance, rhyme, draw, scribble and giggle — anything to facilitate learning the concepts the children need to learn. In many third grades, the focus shifts. Incoming third graders are expected to have the tools to tackle curriculum content. In order to do so, they should:

- read well enough to read and comprehend all content areas.
- be able to work independently.
- be comfortable working in a cooperative learning group.
- be able to sustain attention for a 25- to 30-minute teacher-directed lesson.
- have good number sense and be able to learn the times-table with ease.
- be able to transfer information from textbooks to paper.
- begin to write in cursive without mixing manuscript.
- begin to tell time to the minute.

The teacher may find herself teaching a "high-pressure" grade level. First and third grades are particularly demanding on a teacher. It is in first grade that formal reading and writing instruction begins. In today's public school systems, a lot of pressure falls onto first grade teachers to have children reading 10 to 12 weeks into the school year.

Third grade is a transitional grade — a bridge between second and fourth grades. It's here that children learn their times tables. Fourth, fifth, and sixth grade teachers report that students who don't know their times tables are in terrible shape for all future math instruction.

A teacher moving up a grade level may find that her class size increases. Most school systems have class size guidelines that vary by grade level. Generally speaking, the lower the grade level, the smaller the class size. Many kindergarten teachers have opted to remain in their kindergarten class, rather than see their class size increase.

Long-Term Relationships — Long-Term Impact

Stephen Parker is a personal counselor who attended a small elementary school in rural New England, and who had the same teacher from first through fourth grade, from 1958 to 1962. He felt moved to talk about his experiences after hearing discussions about looping and long-term teacher-student relationships.

Parker's teacher, Mrs. Johnson*, taught reading, writing, spelling, arithmetic, music, and art to students in four different grades in the same room — a total of about 30 children. Parker's class size varied, but generally numbered around six.

"Mrs. Johnson could teach an inanimate object to read," Parker said.

Mrs. Johnson encouraged her young students to do a lot of creative writing, and used a mimeograph machine to run off stories the children had written; she encouraged, but didn't require, students to read their stories aloud and take pride in them, and made them into booklets so that they would feel like authors.

"She taught phonics too, and it worked. Even the 'slower' students learned to read quite well." By the end of first grade/beginning of second grade, Parker's reading skills were tested at twelfth-grade level. "Even the kids who were considered 'slow' were testing at sixth grade level," Parker said.

One way she pulled everyone in was to use Dr. Seuss books to teach phonics and reading skills.

"Everybody liked Dr. Seuss; she was a big proponent of Dr. Seuss. I think she knew him," Parker said.

Those students who started off with Mrs. Johnson from the very beginning really thrived, said Parker; she had some success with kids who came into the class in third or fourth grade, but not as much as with her long-term students.

"She should have been a reading specialist," he said. "She obviously had a love for it. She loved watching people blossom, and learn to read, not just by rote, but with expression. 'Are you asking me or telling me?' she'd say when our voices went up at the end of a sentence.

"She was also excellent at teaching art and music. I think it's because of her influence that I like to write, and like music so well." (Parker is knowledgeable to the point of expertise on most forms of music dating from the 1930s to the present.)

"Miss Jean Brodie"

Parker describes Mrs. Johnson as fiery, enigmatic and creative, ahead of her time in terms of language, and in terms of her openness.

---

* Not her real name. "Mrs. Johnson" is still alive, and Parker "wouldn't want to hurt her feelings."

"She had a Jean Brodie quality in that she encouraged us to think in terms of the future, and not assume that everything was going to stay the same. She invited open dialogue and open instruction, encouraged us to stretch the boundaries of our imagination, and didn't limit us."

She would often bring a TV into the classroom and show an educational channel; the students would watch art programs and science programs, for example, when the topics applied. "She exposed us to things we otherwise wouldn't have been exposed to in rural New England at that time."

Mrs. Johnson's daughter taught school in Japan, and visited Parker's school one day and talked about Japan. When Parker was in fourth grade, the class had a substitute for a long period of time while Mrs. Johnson took an extended trip to England; she sent back letters and postcards and photographs, giving her students lots of detailed information about what she was seeing.

Mrs. Johnson also encouraged her students to understand that at some point they were going to be young adults, and that they needed to acquire the skills to conduct themselves as young adults.

Math — the Achilles Heel

Mrs. Johnson was as bad in teaching math as she was expert in teaching language arts. "She didn't seem to have the patience or aptitude for teaching math skills, and didn't want to bother," Parker said. Some students who had a natural aptitude for numbers did fine; for others the experience was very damaging.

Mrs. Johnson was pretty liberal in allowing students special recesses; if you got your work done early, you could go outside. Parker feels it was partly to free herself up to work with specific groups of students without having to worry about others sitting idle.

"I had problems with math, and instead of helping me with it, like she would do with students having problems with language arts, she would just make me stay in and work on it; and I ended up feeling punished."

Parker had another teacher — the only other teacher in the school — in fifth and sixth grades. By that time, the students were very vocal about being allowed to work on their own and work ahead, and the new teacher let them work independently as a group.

"The problem was, where some students had shortcomings, the other students would cheat for them, because we didn't want to go back to a more structured environment. I virtually ignored math. I didn't learn a stitch of math after third grade—not a stitch. By the time I was in seventh grade I was math-illiterate."

The Dark Side of Miss Jean Brodie

Mrs. Johnson was a controversial figure — high-tempered (she used to bounce chalkboard erasers off kids' heads if they weren't paying attention), and at times caustic. Being one of only two teachers in the school, with no real direct day-to-day supervision, she had free rein, just like the Jean Brodie character.

"She could be militaristic with people who were shy or introverted; rather than drawing them out, she would try to force them out, sometimes to the point of humiliating them.

"Especially the state kids." There was one family in the small town that took in a lot of foster kids; Mrs. Johnson seemed to have the attitude that they were not as substantial or acceptable as the rest of the children.

"She drove them harder, to the point where she was reminding them of cultural disadvantages.

"A very important component of the school experience was that we had these culturally disadvantaged students. Whether she knew she was doing it or not, she was teaching us to draw a line, to create a caste system, and because we wanted to be in favor, we fell into line like little soldiers, even though as a young seven-year-old I felt it was inappropriate. Underneath, we all knew it was wrong.

"I think Mrs. Johnson was blind to her prejudices. Maybe she was frustrated, because she didn't know how to get through to these kids.

"She was a paradox; she wanted to teach holistically, but she didn't want to be saddled with dealing with the psychology of the individual student."

Mrs. Johnson had personal problems; her husband had died the year before Parker entered first grade, and the teacher may have been recovering from grief and anger at the man's death. For whatever reason, she put a lot of emotional content into her dealings with her students and sometimes it was destructive. "Anyone that ever experienced her had the same feelings," Parker said.

"Except for the state kids. They went away with a different, much more negative perspective.

"I always felt I was being a hypocrite, because I was adopted; I was secretly just like them. I mean, we played with these kids; how could they be any different than us? Some of their actions that were negative were because we were being taught to treat them with pity or disdain.

"I felt tremendously guilty because of my adoption, even though the teacher didn't take an attitude toward me because of it. She knew my parents, and associated with them at church and through various town activities. I felt like I was a big secret, like an impostor; and her prejudices fed into that. They were pushing me back up against the wall and constantly questioning every attitude I had.

"She was overlooking the life that I, and the other students, had outside of school, and wasn't addressing life's issues positively.

"I think she drove the state kids hard trying to make them rise above their situation; she thought she was doing them a favor. Meanwhile, I was terrified of taking on the behaviors of some of the negative students. I developed a real phobia about it, to the point where I didn't want to go to school."

Long Term Effects

Parker realized in discussing Mrs. Johnson that a lot of the atmosphere and a lot of the way he was taught reflects the way he handles things now. "I can see a lot of her influence in my personality," he said. "Some of the inconsistencies that were present in the educational system have been carried through in most of my adult life, and have had a big effect on me." His teacher's treatment of other students, for instance, brought out a certain level of elitism. "I was taught to feel very elite and superior in certain ways in terms of skills I was proficient in, and like the dregs in the areas where I was foundering.

"I was both praised in a major way and rewarded handsomely for my verbal skills, and chastised gravely for my deficiency in math. I fell back on what worked and shunned what didn't, and developed a rift between the two so that there's a real gap in my abilities. It creates a stalemate where you have all this potential — I can read *A Brief History of Time* by Stephen Hawking and understand the concepts, which are scientific tending toward the metaphysical, and yet I blocked myself from developing the basic mechanical skills necessary to learning basic algebra and the steps leading to participating in the academic process of physics and other math and science subjects."

It's not surprising that Mrs. Johnson had so strong an influence on her students, said Parker, when you consider that "we spent most of our waking hours with her for four years."

Parker's Thoughts on Looping

"There has to be some real care taken with this concept called looping," Parker said. "There needs to be some consistency in the feedback the child is receiving, both positive and negative. With a basically intelligent student you have to be really careful in how you handle criticism."

He also feels that the lack of direct supervision fed into the freewheeling way Mrs. Johnson approached her students, and allowed her power that could at times be harmful.

"In many ways she was an excellent teacher, and her openness and futuristic outlook gave us the exaggerated belief that you can do anything; that you just go out and do it." That belief can be valuable, but as Parker said, "with so many gaps in knowledge it becomes destructive."

Summer Learning

Multiyear teachers who've been at it for awhile are finding that extending the learning over the summer months, by assigning reading or other projects between the first and second school years, helps continue the momentum into the second year and provides even more continuity for the students. Frank Leary, principal of Cyril K. Brennan Middle School in Attleboro, Massachusetts, says,

> One of the big pieces of the two-year model has to be the summer maintenance program in between the two years, and what can be offered to maintain some of the things the students have learned. When you first begin [the multiyear assignment] you don't think a summer program is an important component of it, but as you get more involved or committed, you realize that it's very important.

A looping classroom with a good summer program can have many of the same benefits, in terms of continuity and momentum, as a year-round school. However, whereas year-round schooling is a major reform requiring a lot of selling to the teaching staff and the public, looping classrooms are a simple reform, and summer programs are as simple as informing parents and students that "there's going to be a little homework over the summer."

Plus, gauging from the samples presented here, most teachers seem to develop summer programs that involve "fun stuff."

The following pages contain some fun stuff that several multiyear teachers have developed for their classrooms. Karen Rettig, a 1-2 looping teacher in Liberty Center, Ohio, has sent two three-month calendars full of summer activities — one for kindergartners who will be entering her first grade, the other for children transitioning from her first grade to her second grade.

Char Forsten, a former multiyear teacher of grades 3-4, 5-6, and 3-4-6[1] at Dublin Consolidated School in Dublin, New Hampshire, assigned summer reading and other projects as well as sending individualized packets home with her students. Her contribution, "The Multiyear Student-Teacher Connection: The Summer Bridge," is an excerpt from her new book, *The Multiyear Lesson Plan Book*.

Glenn Killough, 3-4 teacher from Joseph Finberg Elementary School in Attleboro, Massachusetts, gives some advice on beginning a program in "A Summer Program for Multiyear Assignments."

---

[1] Forsten had her students for grades three and four, then got them back after fifth grade.

Summer Projects
Incoming First Grade Students

Summer Brainwork to Exercise Your Mind

Dear Parents,

The attached calendars are for you to use to keep those skills and minds in working order and help the children have a successful start in first grade.

Please put a star or smile face in each of the boxes of the activities you do. The calendars that are returned to us in the fall during the first week, with at least 10 marks per month will be rewarded with a surprise. The calendar with the most marks will receive a special surprise.

Please sign each page to authenticate the activities done. The activities do not need to be returned, just the calendars.

Thank you for your support and enjoy your summer.

Your Future First Grade Teachers

Kathy Bishop, Karen Rettig and Dawn Sharpe

Summer Projects
Incoming First Grade Students

JUNE

Sunday	Monday	Tuesday	Wednesday	Thursday	Friday	Saturday
				1 Tell someone what month begins today.	**2** Find 2 things that begin with the letter a.	**3**
4	**5** Count as far as you can to someone.	**6** Find 2 things that begin with the letter b. Ask someone to spell them to you.	**7** Show someone what a penny is and tell them how much it is worth.	**8** Look in a magazine, book or newspaper for 2 words that begin with c.	**9** Have someone read your favorite book today!	**10**
11	**12** Practice writing your alphabet in your neatest handwriting.	**13** Draw 2 pictures of something that starts with the letter d. Ask someone to spell them.	**14** Today is Flag Day. Tell someone what Flag Day is or ask them what it is.	**15** Elephant & egg begin with e. Tell someone a story about an elephant and an egg.	**16** Make a Father's Day Card to give to your dad on Sunday.	**17**
18 Tell your dad that you love him and Happy Father's Day!	**19** Find 2 things that begin with the letter f.	**20** Tell someone the days of the week.	**21** Play outside if the weather is nice and enjoy the first day of summer!	**22** Find 2 pictures of things that begin with the letter g.	**23** Tell someone you love them today.	**24**
25	**26** Happy Monday! Have a great day!	**27** Draw 2 pictures of things that begin with h.	**28** Make a pattern for someone.	**29** I is at the beginning of the word igloo. What is an igloo? Would you like to be in one today?	**30** Enjoy the last day of June! Tell someone what month begins tomorrow.	

Parent's Signature _____

123

Summer Projects
Incoming First Grade Students

JULY

Sunday	Monday	Tuesday	Wednesday	Thursday	Friday	Saturday
						1
2	**3** How many days does July have? Can you find another month w/ the same number of days?	**4** Happy Fourth of July!	**5** What letter does July begin with? Can you find two other months that begin w/ the same letter?	**6** Tell someone 2 summer safety rules. We hope you are using them and will continue to.	**7** Find 2 things that begin with k at your house. Ask someone to spell them for you.	**8**
9	**10** Sing a song to someone. One you know or one you made up.	**11** Love begins with the letter L. Make a card for someone you love.	**12** Tell someone a way you were helpful this week.	**13** Draw 2 things that begin with the letter m. Ask someone to spell them.	**14** Practice writing your name in your best handwriting.	**15**
16	**17** Think of 3 words that rhyme with cat.	**18** Look in a magazine or book and find two things that begin with n.	**19** Tell someone your favorite flavor of ice cream.	**20** O is for Ollie the Octopus. Dictate a story to someone about Ollie the Octopus.	**21** Count backwards from 10. Can you do it from 20?	**22**
23	**24** Sometime this week see if you can catch a lightening bug. Why does it light up?	**25** P is for pattern. Make a pattern for someone.	**26** Answer these math problems. $1 + 2 = $ ___ $2 + 0 = $ ___ $2 + 3 = $ ___ $3 + 1 = $ ___ $3 + 3 = $ ___	**27** Q is for quarter. How much is a quarter? See if you can find one.	**28** Tell someone what today is. Did you say the month, day and year?	**29**
30	**31** Happy last day of July! Have a great Monday!					

Parent's Signature _____

124

Summer Projects
Incoming First Grade Students

AUGUST

Sunday	Monday	Tuesday	Wednesday	Thursday	Friday	Saturday
		1 Sometime this week, go to school and see who your teacher will be.	**2** Find 2 things that begins with r. Ask someone to spell them for you.	**3** Sometime this week clean your room. Don't forget to clean under your bed!!	**4** Draw 2 things that begin with s. Ask someone to spell them for you.	**5**
6	**7** Say your address and phone number to someone at your house.	**8** Find 2 words in a magazine or paper that begin with t.	**9** Look for the big dipper tonight.	**10** U is for umbrella. Do you need one today?	**11** Practice writing your numbers today.	**12**
13	**14** How many days until you get to see all of your friends again?	**15** V is for vase. Draw a picture of a vase with flowers.	**16** Help your parents test the smoke detectors in your house with the test button.	**17** Find 2 pictures or words that begin with w.	**18** Give all of your family hugs today!	**19**
20	**21** X is in the word eXcellent. We hope you have an excellent day!	**22** Practice writing the alphabet today.	**23** Y is for yesterday. What day was yesterday?	**24** Have a super day!	**25** Z is for zebra. Tell someone how you think the zebra got its stripes.	**26**
27	**28** Get a good night's rest for the first day of school tomorrow.	**29** We look forward to seeing your bright and smiling face today!	**30** Have a super day at school!	**31** Tell your parents two things that you did at school today!		

Parent's Signature _____

125

Summer Projects
Incoming First to Second Grade Students

Summer Brainwork to Exercise Your Mind

Parents,

The attached calendars are for you to use to keep those skills and minds in working order. Please put a star or smile face in each of the boxes of the activities you do. The calendars that are returned to us in the fall during the first week, with at least 10 marks per month will be rewarded with a surprise. The calendar with the most marks will receive a special surprise.

Please sign each page to authenticate the activities done. The activities do NOT need to be returned, just the calendars.

Also in your child's bookbag is a packet of old worksheets, extra workbook pages, and other miscellaneous pages that were found on our shelves. Please ration these out through the course of the summer to keep our brains in working order.

Your Future First Grade Teachers

Kathy Bishop, Karen Rettig and Dawn Sharpe

Summer Projects
Incoming First to Second Grade Students

JUNE

Sunday	Monday	Tuesday	Wednesday	Thursday	Friday	Saturday
			1 Tell someone what month begins today.	**2** Listen to a cricket chirp. What do you think it says?	**3** Tell someone 3 summer safety rules. Please use them during the summer! Thanks!	**4**
5	**6** Sometime this week see if you can catch a lightening bug. Why does it light up?	**7** Tell someone how much money is 2 quarters.	**8** Count the number of eyes in your house. (Remember to count by 2). Write the answer here. ___	**9** Tell someone what you ate from the fruit group today.	**10** Read your favorite book today!	**11**
12	**13** Write 3 words that rhyme with cat.	**14** Today is Flag Day. Tell someone what the American Flag means to you.	**15** Happy Wednesday! Have a fun day!	**16** Count by 10's as far as you can to someone	**17** Make a Father's Day Card to give to your dad on Sunday.	**18**
19 Tell your dad that you love him and Happy Father's Day!	**20** Tell someone 5 things that you can do with your hands.	**21** Play outside if the weather is nice and enjoy the first day of summer	**22** Tell someone the 12 months of the year.	**23** Tell someone a way you can make 15 cents.	**24** Tell someone 2 nice things you did today.	**25**
26	**27** Tell someone 3 things that can be recycled.	**28** Look at the clock. Tell someone what time it is right now.	**29** Write the answers: 5 + 5 = ___ 6 + 8 = ___ 15 - 7 = ___	**30** Enjoy the last day of June!		

Parent's Signature _____

Summer Projects
Incoming First to Second Grade Students

JULY

Sunday	Monday	Tuesday	Wednesday	Thursday	Friday	Saturday
					1 How many days does July have? Which other months have the same number of days?	**2**
3	**4** Happy Fourth of July!	**5** Count as far as you can in Spanish	**6** Say 3 ways you can make 25 cents.	**7** Count by 5's as high as you can.	**8** Write a nice note to someone that lives at your house.	**9**
10	**11** Draw a clock on scrap paper, make it show 6:30.	**12** Make and give your parents an award.	**13** Tell someone about a book you just read.	**14** Count the pairs of shoes in your house. How many shoes is that total? (Count by 2's)	**15** Sing a song to someone. One you know or one you made up.	**16**
17	**18** Sometime this week write a story about your favorite thing you did so far this summer.	**19** Add together the ages of all the people that live at your house.	**20** Tell someone a way that you were helpful this week.	**21** Play tic tac toe with all of the people in your house.	**22** Have a great Friday!	**23**
24	**25** Tell someone what your favorite thing was that you did over the weekend.	**26** Estimate how far it would be to walk 30 huge steps. Check to see how close you were.	**27** Think of 4 words that rhyme with star.	**28** Count the number of toes in your family. Did you count by 5's or 10's?	**29** Tell someone your favorite ice cream flavor.	**30**
						31

Parent's Signature _____

Summer Projects
Incoming First to Second Grade Students

AUGUST

Sunday	Monday	Tuesday	Wednesday	Thursday	Friday	Saturday
	1 Make a goal for the new school year! It will be here before we know it!	**2** Find as many different leaves that you can. See if you or someone can identify them.	**3** Say and write 5 words that have silent letters.	**4** How much is 3 dimes, 2 nickels and 4 pennies?	**5** Clean your room. Clean under your bed also.	**6**
7	**8** Ask your parents if you can write a letter and mail it to someone.	**9** If you can, mail your letter today.	**10** Say your address and phone number to someone at your house.	**11** Add the numbers in your phone number.	**12** Tell someone 2 contractions and what words make them up.	**13**
14	**15** Sometime this month look in your mailbox for a special letter.	**16** Have a wonderful day!	**17** Tell someone how many more days until school will begin.	**18** Tell someone what you ate from the vegetable group today.	**19** Look for the Big Dipper tonight.	**20**
21	**22** Tell all of the people in your house that you love them.	**23** How many days until you get to see all of your friends again?	**24** Help your parents test the smoke detectors in your house with the test button.	**25** Give all of your family hugs today.	**26** Enjoy your last summer Friday!	**27**
28 Get a good night's rest for your 1st day back at school!	**29** I am looking forward to seeing your bright and smiling face today!	**30**	**31**			

Parent's Signature _____

The Multiyear Student-Teacher Connection:
"The Summer Bridge"

Summer Activities that Bridge the Years . . .
(parents can fill out charts for younger students)

- **Summer Reading & Reflective Journals:**
  — Use the Summer Reading Log in this section for students to record the books they read over the summer. Ask them to return it in the fall.

- **Summer Projects in Nature, Photography, Art, Music, Plays:**
  — Many students pursue interesting hobbies and activities in the summer. Ask them to record them on the Project Chart to share with the class.

- **Making Connections** (Connecting learning with the real world)
  — Use the Scavenger Hunt Chart to keep track of real-world connections.

- **Corresponding** (Student/Teacher postcards . . . to keep in touch)

- **Goal-setting** (Reflect over first year, set goals for second year)

- **Individualized Review & Extensions:**
  — Put together customized packets of lessons or materials that students can work on independently, or that parents can use to help their students maintain or continue progress.

A Special Note: Who are your at-risk students? Who needs customized summer learning to continue their educational momentum? I believe that all students benefit from seeing education as a life-long learning process. When you teach in a multiyear cycle, you have the distinct advantage of staying connected and making connections. You can build "summer bridges" that link the years in your unique multiyear program. What those "bridges" are will depend on you and your students' needs. You can provide ongoing lessons for "at-risk" students to do at home to minimize "losing ground" over the summer. Reading logs, projects, and correspondence ideas are all summer options that are simple, fun and effective. Make your summer links creative and meaningful, emphasizing that what they learn and discover on their own is a powerful component in their education.

Char Forsten. Society For Developmental Education.

_____'s Summer Bridge

Student's Name

SUMMER READING LOG

Directions: Record your summer reading in the chart below. Parents can help!

Title	Author	Date	Comments

Summer Project(s)

Completed by: _____

My special summer project was: _____
_____

I used these materials: _____
_____

Some things I learned: _____
_____

What I liked best about this project: _____
_____

I would like to learn more about:
_____

_____

SUMMER CONNECTIONS:

Summer Scavenger Hunt . . . Making Real-World Connections:

Directions: During the school year, we explored the world around us for examples of shapes, numbers, symmetry, mixtures, solutions, and other math and science topics. We also looked for objects that our vocabulary words described. Become a summer scavenger! Continue to look for interesting examples of what we have studied. When you find something, ask your parent to list it or write it yourself in the chart below.

Examples:	What I Saw	Where I Saw It	Comments
Math:			
Science:			
Nouns:			
Adjectives:			
Other:			

Char Forsten. Society For Developmental Education.

A Summer Program for Multiyear Assignments

by Glenn Killough

Starting a summer program for your students between the school years has many benefits. Educationally it offers the opportunity to explore and discover more than during the confines of the school year, and emotionally it helps to strengthen the child/teacher/class bond.

The idea of a summer program came to me in February during the first year of a multiyear (grade three to grade four) assignment. The thought of being able to "keep the ball rolling" during the summer recess seemed a logical and educationally sound idea.

I feel that to get a group of nine-and ten-year-olds to do anything in the summer they have to have ownership of it. I first polled the class to see if interest was high enough to justify the time that would be needed for the steps to follow. I used the, "If you could . . . what would you do?" approach to present the idea. The concept was well-received by the class and we went on to lay the foundation of the program.

The class decided that one meeting a week for six weeks would be enough. The starting time would be 8:30 am and the ending time would be 12:30 pm. Meeting one day a week kept the feeling of the school alive. If we had gone for say, five days in succession, one of my goals would not have been met: that was to keep the spirit of class unity going for the entire two-year run that I would have these children.

When the initial brainstorming was complete, I drafted a proposal to the central administration (through my principal, of course) requesting funding for the program. So as not to strain the school district's budget, after discussions with the administration, I decided that a nominal materials fee would be charged each student. Once approval was received I went about the task of planning the weekly activities. (I have to point out that it is most important to keep your parents informed of plans as they develop. Parents are our biggest supporters. Without the parents behind you, a program like this will not work.)

To come up with ideas, the class and I again brainstormed things that would be of interest to them. This gave me a starting point for research. I chose science as the thrust for this particular group of students (based on our brainstorming). We decided social studies and geography would also be fun areas to explore.

As a kickoff we went on a field trip to a science museum. I opened the trip to parents and had an overwhelming response from them. (Almost as many parents as children went!) The next weeks we collected and studied field insects, pond/water life, and weather/temperature. I found that the flexibility of an uninterrupted block of time enabled free observation, exploration and discovery. During the pond life/water life week so many questions were generated that we extended it to three weeks.

Our normal day started with an overview of the planned activities. We then went about the activities. A snack break was held, then a discussion of the first part of the day. We then played a game that encouraged team building and cooperation, and finished with time in our computer lab to keep skills sharp and to record the day in a computer journal.

Here are some tips to help you plan a summer program:

- Present your plan to administrators.
- Plan with your class. Keep them involved!
- Communicate with parents. Keep them informed!
- Have activities that are out of the normal realm of what you do.
- Be flexible in your plans to allow students to "run" with topics.

If you choose to try a summer program, *good luck!* I'm sure you will find it as rewarding as I did.

CHAPTER 11

Retention — A High-Stakes Decision

One of the most critical decisions a teacher has to make is whether to promote or retain a child who is not succeeding in school. While looping certainly reduces the need for grade-level retention, it does not entirely eliminate it. The issue of whether to retain or socially promote a student is difficult, and is made more so because of its controversial and sometimes political nature. The National Association for the Education of Young Children (NAEYC) has taken a position against not only grade-level retention, but any form of extra time if it exceeds the traditional lock-step time frame. Many studies have been made that show negative consequences of retaining students. (On the other side, many school systems have rigid retention policies that require students to be retained based on a single factor, such as a standardized test score.)

While social promotion may be done partly to save a student the embarrassment and emotional pain of being left behind by his peers, the decision is often an economic one; that is, the school system doesn't want to pay for an extra year of schooling.

We're Retaining the Wrong Kids!

Most of the studies made on retention have two problems: they're group studies, rather than individual case studies, and they're made on a population which includes many students retained for the wrong reasons. Naturally, the results are going to be skewed.

When Retention is an Inappropriate Intervention

The children who are retained exhibit real problems that need to be addressed somehow. But many times grade-level retention is used when another intervention would be more appropriate and more effective. For the following students, retention may well be counterproductive:

- *The slower learner.* A child with a low I.Q. a (range of 70-89), who has been identified as a slower learner, usually will not benefit much from an extra year of the same curriculum with the same teacher. A more appropriate intervention may be a special-needs assessment and instructional support and adaptations as needed. Retention is not a substitute for special education!

- *An unmotivated student.* An unmotivated student will certainly not be motivated by another year of the same curriculum that bored him in the first place. Better to recognize the problem early and try to fix it; learning contracts may help, as well as thematic studies that incorporate some of the unmotivated student's interests.

If the student doesn't respond to coaching or encouragement whatsoever, it might be wise to look at underlying causes for the lack of motivation.

•   *An emotionally disturbed child.* Counseling, and in some severe cases, special placement, would be more appropriate than grade-level retention. Retention in this case may only add more pressure and stress to the child's life.

Be aware that some children show signs of emotional distress when they are in over their heads academically or socially in school. This is a readiness issue, which *can* usually be addressed by more learning time in a grade.

•   *A child with a behavior disorder.* Again, counseling, and possibly a different approach to in-class rules of behavior would be appropriate.

•   *A child raised in poverty.* Enrichment activities, acceleration, and tutoring may be more appropriate to make up for a lack of resources at home. (Be aware that a background of poverty often creates readiness issues.)

•   *A linguistically different child.* A child who cannot understand what's going on in class because of a language barrier is not going to understand it the second time around, without help. A better intervention would be a good ESL (English as a Second Language) program which supports the child's studies while teaching the child English.

•   *A child who has a history of excessive absenteeism.* This is a usually a parental issue, not the child's issue, and needs to be worked out with the parents or guardian.

Sometimes excessive absenteeism may be because the child's family moves frequently. Grade-level retention won't help here; possibly assessment of academic needs and individualized instruction and tutoring might. This is a tough issue. Teachers have to reconcile themselves to doing the best they can with transient students while they have them and, unfortunately, let go when the students are gone. (An aside—if outgoing students can be packed off with lots of authentic assessment of their capabilities for their next teacher, they will have a head start on their next school assignment.)

A long period of absence caused by a student's illness, or injury in an accident, is different. Grade-level retention may be appropriate under these circumstances depending on the length of the student's absence from school.

•   *A child whose parents are opposed to extra time through grade-level retention.* Parents have very strong feelings about retention, on both sides of the issue. Some parents will be very adamant about their child's not staying back. Forced retention against parents' wishes never works.

•   *A child who is already a year older than his peers.* Placing a child in a single-grade classroom with children two years younger than he will isolate him from children his own age and create a peer group for him that is very much younger than him developmentally. The child's self-esteem will suffer.

Students who are much older than their classmates are at high risk for dropping out of school.

•   *A child who is too "street wise" for her age.* This is for the benefit of the children coming into the class — they don't need to learn what this student can teach them; and retention will not bring this student back to an age of innocence.

•   *A child who has a multitude of complex problems (high-impact child).* When a child is exposed to many risk factors — for instance, coming from poverty, from a single-parent family, with health problems — each problem interacts with every other problem, making each one impact more strongly on the child. A grade-level retention for such a highly-impacted child will probably add more stress to an already burdensome situation. This child and his or her family need to be connected with as many support services as necessary.

• *A child with very low self-esteem.* This child could be devastated by grade-level retention. Often it is better to socially promote, while supporting the child's academics and social/emotional needs.

Be aware of the fact that children placed in the wrong grade exhibit signs of low self-esteem. Assess the child's developmental readiness and current grade placement; if it is determined that a lack of readiness is the issue here, moving the child back to a lower grade, or retaining the child, may solve the problem.

Retention and Readiness

Grade-level retention is most often the appropriate intervention to correct wrong grade placement. A good candidate for retention may be:

- chronologically too young for his/her present grade-level placement.
- developmentally too young for his/her grade or program.
- physically small for his or her age.

The child should be of average or above-average intelligence, without apparent learning disabilities, and be in the same age range as his or her current peer group (within a year of being the same age.)

The parents must strongly support grade-level retention for their child, and the child must be able to accept it as well. (In some instances, children have asked to be allowed to stay in the same grade for a second year; this request should be honored if possible.)

Do It Early

If a child needs more time in a grade, do it in the early childhood years — and don't hesitate to change a child's placement midyear if necessary. When a child is in the wrong grade, it's evident from the outset. Making a child struggle through three years of schooling and delaying a decision to retain until third grade will cause the child years of unnecessary frustration, and will batter his or her self-esteem. Retention on top of all this will be a hard blow.

If you do have to retain an older student, do it only with his or her unconditional support.

Negative Impact on Children Who are in Over Their Heads in the Wrong Grade

They may:

- exhibit behavior problems.
- have difficulty paying attention.
- have difficulty learning routine tasks.
- have high absenteeism.
- have low academic performance.
- feel hurried/harried/stressed.
- be depressed.
- have a poor self-concept.
- be easily discouraged.
- have low stamina both physically and emotionally.
- display emotional problems.
- have difficulty socially.
- in extreme cases have self-destructive behaviors.

Many of these children require remedial and counseling services as a direct result of being in the wrong grade.

Making the Decision

Don't ever make a decision to retain a student unilaterally. This decision should involve the classroom teacher, the principal, any support staff and specialists involved, and the parents.

The decision to retain should be made based on many factors, not on a single test score or some other isolated event. Where another, less drastic intervention may resolve a student's school problems, that strategy should be used.

Retention Plus

Keeping a student in the same grade for two years will not magically solve the student's academic problems. A teacher needs to explore instructional strategies that will work better with this student than the ones that failed the student the previous year. (If a particular approach didn't work the first time, it probably won't work the second.)

Make sure that remedial and support services are provided as needed. Be aware that, even if a child is retained because of a readiness issue, he or she may have other difficulties, like learning problems, that need to be addressed.

Looping and Retention

As we said at the beginning of the chapter, looping can reduce, but not eliminate grade-level retention. The advantage of looping is that the teacher has two years to observe and get to know each student, two years to identify and assess potential problems, and two years to implement instructional strategies and apply interventions to resolve any problems that may exist.

With borderline students — those students who may not need a full year, but just a little extra time and attention — that may be enough. When developmentally young students have serious difficulty after two years in a multiyear classroom, grade-level retention should be considered when, and only when, all other options have been tried. Retention is a necessary tool, but it should be the intervention of last resort.

BIBLIOGRAPHY

Looping and Related Topics

Burke, Daniel L. "Multi-Year Teacher/Student Relationships Are a Long-Overdue Arrangement," *Phi Delta Kappan*, January 1996.

ERS Info-File #285.0. "Persistence Teams/Looping." This is a collection of articles about multiyear assignments and related topics; many of the articles are about Waldorf schools. Contact: Educational Research Service, 2000 Clarendon Blvd., Arlington VA 22201 Phone: 703-243-2100; FAX 703-243-8316; e-mail: ers@access.digex.net

Forsten, Char. *The Multiyear Lesson Plan Book*. Peterborough, NH: Crystal Springs Books, 1996.

George, Paul S.; Spruel, Melody; and Moorefield, Jane. *Lincoln Middle School; A Case Study in Long-term Relationships*. Columbus, OH: National Middle School Association, 1987.

Grant, Jim. *The Looping Classroom*. (Video) Peterborough, NH: Crystal Springs Books, 1996. Two versions: one for teachers and administrators, and one for parents.

Hanson, Barbara. "Getting to Know You: Multiyear Teaching," *Educational Leadership*, November, 1995.

Jacoby, Deborah. "Twice the Learning and Twice the Love." *Teaching K-8*, March 1994.

Mazzuchi, Diana, and Brooks, Nancy. "The Gift of Time." *Teaching K-8*, February, 1992.

Million, June. "To Loop or Not to Loop? This is a Question for Many Schools." NAESP Communicator, Vol. 18, Number 6, February 1996.

Rappa, Joseph B. "Presentation to the National Education Commission on Time and Learning," Cambridge, MA, September 24, 1993. Available from the Attleboro, Massachusetts School District (508-222-0012).

Other Topics of Interest to Multiyear Teachers

Assessment

Batzle, Janine. *Portfolio Assessment and Evaluation: Developing and Using Portfolios in the K-6 Classroom*. Cypress, CA: Creative Teaching Press, 1992.

Belanoff, Pat, and Dickson, Marcia, eds. *Portfolios: Process and Product*. Portsmouth, NH: Heinemann, 1991.

Clay, Marie. *An Observation Survey of Early Literacy Achievement*. Portsmouth, NH: Heinemann, 1993.

———. *Sand and Stones: "Concepts about Print" Tests*. Portsmouth, NH: Heinemann, 1980.

Clemmons, J., Laase, L., Cooper, D., Areglado, N., and Dill, M. *Portfolios in the Classroom: A Teacher's Sourcebook*. New York: Scholastic, Inc., 1993.

Daly, Elizabeth, ed. *Monitoring Children's Language Development*. Portsmouth, NH: Heinemann, 1992.

Graves, Donald, and Sustein, Bonnie, eds. *Portfolio Portraits*. Portsmouth, NH: Heinemann, 1992.

Harp, Bill, ed. *Assessment and Evaluation in Whole Language Programs*. Norwood, MA: Christopher Gordon Publishers, 1993.

Lazear, David. *Multiple Intelligence Approaches to Assessment: Solving the Assessment Conundrum*. IRI/Skylight Publishing, Inc., 1994.

Parsons, Les. *Response Journals*. Portsmouth, NH: Heinemann, 1989.

Picciotto, Linda. *Evaluation: A Team Effort*. Ont.: Scholastic, 1992.

Behavior/Discipline

Albert, Linda. *An Administrator's Guide to Cooperative Discipline*. Circle Pines, MN: American Guidance, 1989.

———. *Cooperative Discipline: How to Manage Your Classroom and Promote Self-Esteem*. Circle Pines, MN: American Guidance Service, 1996.

———. *Cooperative Discipline Elementary Kit*. (three-video series, Implementation Guide, ten color posters, Cooperative Discipline book). Circle Pines, MN: American Guidance Service, 1996.)

———. *Linda Albert's Advice for Coping With Kids*. Tampa, FL: Alkorn House, 1992.

———. *Responsible Kids in School and At Home: The Cooperative Discipline Way*. (six-video series). Circle Pines, MN: American Guidance Service, 1994.

Bluestein, Jane. *21st Century Discipline — Teaching Students Responsibility and Self-Control*. New York: Scholastic, 1988.

Burke, Kay. *What to Do with the Kid Who . . . Developing Cooperation, Self-Discipline and Responsibility in the Classroom*. Palatine, IL: IRI/Skylight Publishing, 1992.

Canfield, Jack, and Siccone, Frank. *101 Ways to Develop Student Self-Esteem and Responsibility*. Needham Heights, MA: Allyn & Bacon, 1993.

Charles, C.M. *Building Classroom Discipline*. New York: Longman, 1992.

Coletta, Anthony. *What's Best for Kids: A Guide to Developmentally Appropriate Practices for Teachers & Parents of Children Ages 4-8*. Rosemont, NJ: Modern Learning Press, 1991.

Curwin, Richard L., and Mendler, Allen N. *Discipline with Dignity*. Alexandria, VA: Association for Supervision and Curriculum Development, 1993.

———. *Am I in Trouble? Using Discipline to Teach Young Children Responsibility*. Santa Cruz, CA: Network Publications, 1990.

Fox, Lynn. *Let's Get Together*. Rolling Hills, CA: Jalmar Press, 1993.

Knight, Michael et al. *Teaching Children to Love Themselves*. Hillside, NJ: Vision Press, 1982.

Kohn, Alfie. *Punished by Rewards: The Trouble with Gold Stars, Incentive Plans, A's, Praise, and Other Bribes*. Boston: Houghton Mifflin, 1993.

Kreidler, William. *Creative Conflict Resolution: Strategies for Keeping Peace in the Classroom*. Glenview, IL: Scott, Foresman, & Co., 1984.

Mendler, Allen. *Smiling at Yourself: Educating Young Children About Stress and Self-Esteem*. Santa Cruz, CA: Network Publications, 1990.

———. *What Do I Do When? How to Achieve Discipline with Dignity in the Classroom*. Bloomington, IL: National Educational Service, 1992.

Nelson, Jane. *Positive Discipline*. New York: Ballantine Books, 1987.

Nelson, Jane; Lott, Lynn; and Glenn, Stephen. *Positive Discipline in the Classroom*. Rocklin, CA: Prima Publishing, 1993.

Redenbach, Sandi. *Self-Esteem: The Necessary Ingredient for Success*. Esteem Seminar Publications, 1991.

Reider, Barbara. *A Hooray Kind of Kid*. Folsom, CA: Sierra House Publishing, 1988.

Vail, Priscilla. *Emotion: The On-Off Switch for Learning*. Rosemont, NJ: Modern Learning Press, 1994.

Wright, Esther. *Good Morning, Class — I Love You!* Rolling Hills, CA: Jalmar Press, 1988.

———. *Loving Discipline A to Z*. San Francisco: Teaching From the Heart, 1994.

Cooperative Learning

Cohen, Dorothy. *Designing Groupwork: Strategies for the Heterogeneous Classroom*. New York: Teachers College Press, 1994.

Curran, Lorna. *Cooperative Learning Lessons for Little Ones: Literature-Based Language Arts and Social Skills*. San Juan Capistrano, CA: Resources for Teachers, Inc., 1992.

DeBolt, Virginia, with Dr. Spencer Kagan. *Write! Cooperative Learning and The Writing Process*. San Juan Capistrano, CA: Kagan Cooperative Learning, 1994.

Ellis, Susan S., and Whalen, Susan F. *Cooperative Learning: Getting Started*. New York: Scholastic, 1990.

Fisher, Bobbi. *Thinking and Learning Together: Curriculum and Community in a Primary Classroom*. Portsmouth, NH: Heinemann, 1995.

Forte, Imogene, and MacKenzie, Joy. *The Cooperative Learning Guide and Planning Pak for Primary Grades: Thematic Projects and Activities*. Nashville, TN: Incentive Publications, 1992.

Glover, Mary, and Sheppard, Linda. *Not on Your Own: The Power of Learning Together*. New York: Scholastic, 1990.

Johnson, David, and Johnson, Roger. *Cooperation and Competition: Theory and Research*. Edina, MN: Interaction Book Company, 1989.

———. *Learning Together and Alone*. Englewood Cliffs, NJ: Prentice Hall, Inc., 1991.

Kagan, Spencer. *Cooperative Learning*. San Juan Capistrano, CA: Resources for Teachers, Inc., 1994.

Reid, Jo Anne; Forrestal, P.; and Cook, J. *Small Group Learning in the Classroom*. Portsmouth, NH: Heinemann, 1989.

Shaw, Vanston, with Spencer Kagan, Ph.D. *Communitybuilding In the Classroom*. San Juan Capistrano, CA: Kagan Cooperative Learning, 1992.

Slavin, Robert. *Cooperative Learning*. Englewood Cliffs, NJ: Prentice Hall, 1989.

———. *Cooperative Learning*. Boston: Allyn and Bacon, 1995.

Curriculum — Overview

Bredekamp, Sue, and Rosegrant, Teresa, eds. *Reaching Potentials: Appropriate Curriculum and Assessment for Young Children*, Vol. 1. Washington, DC: NAEYC, 1992.

Dodge, Diane Trister; Jablon, Judy R.; and Bickart, Toni S. *Constructing Curriculum for the Primary Grades*. Washington, DC: Teaching Strategies, Inc., 1994.

Fogarty, Robin. *The Mindful School: How to Integrate the Curricula.* Palatine, IL: Skylight Publishing, 1991.

Hall, G.E., and Loucks, S.F. "Program Definition and Adaptation: Implications for Inservice." *Journal of Research and Development in Education* (1981) 14, 2:46-58.

Hohmann, C. *Mathematics: High Scope K-3 Curriculum Guide.* (illustrated field test edition.) Ypsilanti, MI: High Scope Press, 1991.

Maehr, J. *Language and Literacy: High Scope K-3 Curriculum Guide.* (illustrated field test edition.) Ypsilanti, MI: High Scope Press, 1991.

National Association of Elementary School Principals. *Standards for Quality Elementary and Middle Schools: Kindergarten through Eighth Grade.* Alexandria, VA, 1990.

Short, Kathy, and Burke, Carolyn. *Creating Curriculum.* Portsmouth, NH: Heinemann, 1981.

Rowan, Thomas E., and Morrow, Lorna J. *Implementing the K-8 Curriculum and Evaluation Standards: Readings from the "Arithmetic Teacher."* Reston, VA: National Council of Teachers of Mathematics, 1993.

Stevenson, S. Christopher and Carr, Judy F. *Integrated Studies in the Middle School: Dancing Through Walls.* New York: Teachers College Press, 1993.

Whitin, D.; Mills, H.; and O'Keefe, T. *Living and Learning Mathematics: Stories and Strategies for Supporting Mathematical Literacy.* Portsmouth, NH: Heinemann, 1990.

Curriculum — Integrated Activities

Bauer, Karen, and Drew, Rosa. *Alternatives to Worksheets.* Cypress, CA: Creative Teaching Press, 1992.

Beierle, Marlene, and Lynes, Teri. *Book Cooks: Literature-Based Classroom Cooking (4-6).* Cypress, CA: 1992.

Brainard, Audrey, and Wrubel, Denise H. *Literature-Based Science Activities: An Integrated Approach.* New York: Scholastic, 1993.

Bruno, Janet. *Book Cooks: Literature-Based Classroom Cooking. (K-3).* Cypress, CA: Creative Teaching Press, 1991.

Burns, Marilyn. *About Teaching Mathematics.* Sausalito, CA: Math Solutions Publications, 1992.

———. *A Collection of Math Lessons: From Grades 3 Through 6.* White Plains: Cuisinaire Company of America, 1987.

Burns, Marilyn, and Tank, B. *A Collection of Math Lessons: From Grades 1 Through 3.* White Plains: Cuisinaire Company of America, 1987.

Cherkerzian, Diane. *The Complete Lesson Plan Book.* Peterborough, NH: Crystal Springs Books, 1993.

Cochrane, Orin, ed. *Reading Experiences in Science.* Winnipeg, Man.: Peguis, 1985.

Forsten, Char. *Teaching Thinking and Problem Solving in Math.* New York: Scholastic Professional Books, 1992.

———. *Using Calculators is Easy!* New York: Scholastic Professional Books, 1992.

Goin, Kenn; Ripp, Eleanor; and Solomon, Kathleen Nastasi. *Bugs to Bunnies: Hands-on Animal Science Activities for Young Children.* New York: Chatterbox Press, 1989.

Hiatt, Catherine; Wolven, Doug; Botka, Gwen; and Richmond, Jennifer. *More Alternatives to Worksheets.* Cypress, CA: Creative Teaching Press, 1994.

Huck, Charlotte, and Hickman, Janet, eds. *The Best of the Web.* Columbus, OH: Ohio State University, 1982.

Irvine, Joan. *How to Make Pop-ups*. New York: Beech Tree Books, 1987.

———. *How to Make Super Pop-ups*. New York: Beech Tree Books, 1992.

Johnson, Virginia. *Hands-On Math: Manipulative Activities for the Classroom*. Cypress, CA: Creative Teaching Press, Inc., 1994.

Jorgensen, Karen. *History Workshop*. Portsmouth, NH: Heinemann, 1993.

Kohl, MaryAnn, and Potter, Jean. *ScienceArts: Discovering Science Through Art Experiences*. Bellingham, WA: Bright Ring Publishing, 1993.

McCarthy, Tara. *Literature-Based Geography Activities: An Integrated Approach*. New York: Scholastic, 1992.

Ritter, Darlene. *Literature-Based Art Activities (K-3)*. Cypress, CA: Creative Teaching Press, 1992.

———. *Literature-Based Art Activities (4-6)*. Cypress, CA: Creative Teaching Press, 1992.

Rothstein, Gloria Lesser. *From Soup to Nuts: Multicultural Cooking Activities and Recipes*. New York: Scholastic, 1994.

Ruef, Kerry. *The Private Eye. Looking/Thinking by Analogy: A Guide to Developing the Interdisciplinary Mind*. Seattle: The Private Eye Project, 1992.

Spann, Mary Beth. *Literature-Based Multicultural Activities*. New York: Scholastic, 1992.

———. *Literature-Based Seasonal and Holiday Activities*. New York: Scholastic, 1991.

Developmental Education/Readiness

Boyer, Ernest L. *The Basic School: A Community for Learning*. Ewing, NJ: Carnegie Foundation for the Advancement of Learning, 1995.

———. *Ready to Learn: A Mandate for the Nation*. Princeton, NJ: The Foundation for the Advancement of Teaching, 1991.

Brazelton, T. Berry. *To Listen to a Child: Understanding the Normal Problems of Growing Up*. Reading, MA: Addison-Wesley, 1986.

———. *Touchpoints: The Essential Reference. Your Child's Emotional and Behavioral Development*. Reading, MA: Addison-Wesley, 1994.

———. *Working and Caring*. Reading, MA: Addison-Wesley, 1985.

Bredekamp, Sue, ed. *Developmentally Appropriate Practice in Early Childhood Programs Serving Children From Birth Through Age 8*, expanded edition. Washington, DC: National Association for the Education of Young Children, 1987.

Charney, Ruth Sidney. *Teaching Children to Care: Management in the Responsive Classroom*. Greenfield, MA: Northeast Foundation for Children, 1991.

Coletta, Anthony. *Kindergarten Readiness Checklist for Parents*. Rosemont, NJ: Modern Learning Press, 1991.

Elovson, Allanna. *The Kindergarten Survival Book*. Santa Monica, CA: Parent Ed Resources, 1991.

Grant, Jim. *Childhood Should Be a ~~Pressure~~ Precious Time*. (poem anthology) Rosemont, NJ: Modern Learning Press, 1989.

———. *Developmental Education in the 1990's*. Rosemont, NJ: Modern Learning Press, 1991.

———. *"I Hate School!" Some Common Sense Answers for Parents Who Want to Know Why*. Rosemont, NJ: Programs for Education, 1994.

———. *Jim Grant's Book of Parent Pages*. Rosemont, NJ: Programs for Education, 1988.

———. *Worth Repeating: Giving Children a Second Chance at School Success*. Rosemont, NJ: Modern Learning Press, 1989.

Grant, Jim, and Azen, Margot. *Every Parent's Owner's Manuals. (Three-, Four-, Five-, Six-, Seven-Year-Old)*. Rosemont, NJ: Programs for Education.

Hayes, Martha, and Faggella, Kathy. *Think It Through*. Bridgeport, CT: First Teacher Press, 1986.

Healy, Jane M. *Endangered Minds: Why Children Don't Think and What We Can Do About It*. New York: Simon and Schuster, 1990.

———. *Your Child's Growing Mind: A Guide to Learning and Brain Development From Birth to Adolescence*. New York: Doubleday, 1987.

Holt, John. *How Children Fail*. New York: Dell Publishing, 1964, 1982.

Horowitz, Janet, and Faggella, Kathy. *Partners for Learning*. Bridgeport, CT: First Teacher Press, 1986.

Karnofsky, Florence, and Weiss, Trudy. *How To Prepare Your Child for Kindergarten*. Carthage, IL: Fearon Teacher Aids, 1993.

Lamb, Beth, and Logsdon, Phyllis. *Positively Kindergarten: A Classroom-Proven, Theme-based Developmental Guide for the Kindergarten Teacher*. Rosemont, NJ: Modern Learning Press, 1991.

Mallory, Bruce, and New, Rebecca, eds. *Diversity and Developmentally Appropriate Practices: Challenges for Early Childhood Education*. New York: Teachers College Press, 1994.

Miller, Karen. *Ages and Stages: Developmental Descriptions and Activities Birth Through Eight Years*. Chelsea, MA: Telshare Publishing Co., 1985.

National Association of Elementary School Principals. *Early Childhood Education and the Elementary School Principal*. Alexandria, VA: NAESP, 1990.

National Association of State Boards of Education. *Right From the Start: The Report of the NASBE Task Force on Early Childhood Education*. Alexandria, VA: NASBE, 1988.

Northeast Foundation for Children. *A Notebook for Teachers: Making Changes in the Elementary Curriculum*. Greenfield, MA, 1993.

Reavis, George H. *The Animal School*. Rosemont, NJ: Modern Learning Press, 1988.

Singer, Dorothy, and Revenson, Tracy. *How a Child Thinks: A Piaget Primer*. Independence, MO: International University Press, 1978.

Uphoff, James K. *Real Facts From Real Schools: What You're Not Supposed To Know About School Readiness and Transition Programs*. Rosemont, NJ: Modern Learning Press, 1990, 1995.

Uphoff, James, K.; Gilmore, June; and Huber, Rosemarie. *Summer Children: Ready (or Not) for School*. Middletown, OH: The Oxford Press, 1986.

Wood, Chip. *Yardsticks: Children in the Classroom Ages 4-12*. Greenfield, MA: Northeast Foundation for Children, 1994.

Inclusion / Differently-Abled / Learning Disabilities

Dudley-Marling, Curtis. *When School is a Struggle*. New York: Scholastic, 1990.

Bailey, D.B, and Wolery, M. *Teaching Infants and Preschoolers with Handicaps*. Columbus, OH: Merrill, 1984.

Dunn, Kathryn B., and Dunn, Allison B. *Trouble with School: A Family Story about Learning Disabilities*. Rockville, MD: Woodbine House, 1993.

Fagan, S.A.; Graves, D.L.; and Tressier-Switlick, D. *Promoting Successful Mainstreaming: Reasonable Classroom Accommodations for Learning Disabled Students.* Rockville, MD: Montgomery County Public Schools, 1984.

Friend, Marilyn, and Cook, Lynne. "The New Mainstreaming." *Instructor Magazine*, (March 1992): 30-35.

Goodman, Gretchen. *I Can Learn! Strategies and Activities for Gray-Area Children.* Peterborough, NH: Crystal Springs Books, 1995.

———. *Inclusive Classrooms from A to Z: A Handbook for Educators.* Columbus, OH: Teachers' Publishing Group, 1994.

Harwell, Joan. *Complete Learning Disabilities Handbook.* New York: Simon & Schuster, 1989.

Jenkins, J., and Jenkins, L. "Peer Tutoring in Elementary and Secondary Programs." In *Effective Strategies for Exceptional Children*, edited by Meyer, E.L.; Vergason, G.A.; and Whelan, R.J., 335-354, Denver, CO: Love Publishing Co., 1988.

Lang, Greg and Berberich, Chris. *All Children are Special: Creating an Inclusive Classroom.* York, ME: Stenhouse Publishers, 1995.

McGregor, G., and Vogelsberg, R.T. *Transition Needs Assessment for Parents.* Philadelphia, PA: Temple University, 1989.

Perske, R. and Perske, M. *Circle of Friends.* Nashville, TN: Abingdon Press, 1988.

Phinney, Margaret. *Reading with the Troubled Reader.* Portsmouth, NH: Heinemann, 1989.

Rainforth, Beverly; York, Jennifer; and McDonald, Cathy. *Collaborative Teams for Students with Severe Disabilities.* Baltimore: Paul H. Brookes, 1992.

Rhodes, Lynn, and Dudley-Marling, Curtis. *Readers and Writers with a Difference: A Holistic Approach to Teaching Learning Disabled and Remedial Students.* Portsmouth: Heinemann, 1988.

Rosner, Jerome. *Helping Children Overcome Learning Difficulties.* New York: Walker and Co., 1979.

Stainback, S., and Stainback, W. *Curriculum Considerations in Inclusive Classrooms: Facilitating Learning for All Students.* Baltimore: Paul H. Brookes, 1992.

———. *Support Networks for Inclusive Schooling.* Baltimore: Paul H. Brookes, 1990.

Stainback, S, Stainback, W., and Forest, M., eds. *Educating All Students in the Mainstream of Regular Education.* Baltimore: Paul H. Brookes, 1987.

Thousand, J., and Villa, R. "Strategies for Educating Learners with Severe Handicaps Within Their Local Home, Schools and Communities." Focus on Exceptional Children, 23 (3), 1-25, 1990.

Vail, Priscilla. *About Dyslexia.* Rosemont, NJ: Programs for Education, 1990.

———. *Smart Kids with School Problems.* New York: E.P. Dutton, 1987.

Vandercook, T., and York, J. "A Team Approach to Program Development and Support." *In Support Networks for Inclusive Schooling: Interdependent Integrated Education*, edited by Stainback, W. and Stainback, S., 95-122. Baltimore: Paul H. Brookes, 1990.

Villa, R., et al. *Restructuring for Caring and Effective Education: Administrative Strategies for Creating Heterogeneous Schools.* Baltimore: Paul H. Brookes, 1992.

Issues in Education

Erb, Thomas O., and Doda, Nancy M. *Team Organization: Promise — Practices and Possibilities.* Washington, D.C.: National Education Association of the United States, 1989.

Ledell, Marjorie and Arnsparger, Arleen. *How to Deal with Community Criticism of School Change.* Alexandria, VA: Association for Supervision and Curriculum Development, 1993.

National Commission on Excellence in Education. *Nation at Risk: The Full Account.* USA Research Staff (ed.), 1984.

———. *Nation at Risk: The Full Account. 2nd ed.* USA Research Inc. Staff (ed.), 1992.

Rasell, Edith, and Rothstein, Richard, Editors. *School Choice: Examining the Evidence.* Washington, DC: Economic Policy Institute, 1993.

Wortman, Bob, and Matlin, Myna. *Leadership in Whole Language: The Principal's Role.* York, ME: Stenhouse Publishers, 1995.

Language Arts

Atwell, Nancie. *Coming to Know: Writing to Learn in the Middle Grades.* Portsmouth, NH: Heinemann, 1990.

———. *In the Middle: Writing, Reading, and Learning with Adolescents.* Portsmouth, NH: Heinemann, 1987.

Beeler, Terri. *I Can Read! I Can Write! Creating a Print-Rich Environment.* Cypress, CA: Creative Teaching Press, 1993.

Beierle, Marlene, and Lynes, Teri. *Teaching Basic Skills through Literature: A Whole Language Approach for Teaching Reading Skills.* Cypress, CA: Creative Teaching Press, 1993.

Bird, Lois Bridge. *Becoming a Whole Language School: The Fair Oaks Story.* Katonah, NY: Richard C. Owen Publishers, 1989.

Bromley, Karen. *Journalling: Engagements in Reading, Writing, and Thinking.* New York: Scholastic, 1993.

Buros, Jay. *Why Whole Language?* Rosemont, NJ: Programs for Education, 1991.

Butler, Andrea, and Turbill, Jan. *Towards a Reading-Writing Classroom.* Portsmouth, NH: Heinemann, 1984.

Butler, Dorothy. *Cushla and Her Books.* Boston: The Horn Book, 1980.

Calkins, Lucy M. *The Art of Teaching Writing.* Portsmouth, NH: Heinemann, 1986.

———. *Lessons from a Child: On the Teaching and Learning of Writing.* Portsmouth, NH: Heinemann, 1983.

———. *Living Between the Lines.* Portsmouth, NH: Heinemann, 1990.

Clay, Marie. *Becoming Literate.* Portsmouth, NH: Heinemann, 1991.

———. *Observing Young Readers.* Portsmouth, NH: Heinemann, 1982.

———. *Reading Recovery: A Guidebook for Teachers in Training.* Portsmouth, NH: Heinemann, 1993.

Clifford, John. *The Experience of Reading: Louise Rosenblatt and Reader-Response Theory.* Portsmouth, NH: Heinemann, 1991.

Cloonan, Kathryn L. *Sing Me A Story, Read Me a Song (Books I and II).* Beverly Hills, FL: Rhythm & Reading Resources, 1991.

———. *Whole Language Holidays.* (Books I and II). Beverly Hills, FL: Rhythm & Reading Resources, 1992.

Dewey, John. *The Child and the Curriculum* and *The School and Society.* Chicago: Phoenix Books, combined edition, 1956.

Eisele, Beverly. *Managing the Whole Language Classroom: A Complete Teaching Resource Guide for K-6 Teachers.* Cypress, CA: Creative Teaching Press, 1991.

Fairfax, Barbara, and Garcia, Adela. *Read! Write! Publish!* Cypress, CA: Creative Teaching Press, 1992.

Fisher, Bobbi. *Joyful Learning: A Whole Language Kindergarten.* Portsmouth, NH: Heinemann, 1991.

Goodman, Yetta. *How Children Construct Literacy.* Newark, DE: International Reading Association, 1990.

Goodman, Yetta M.; Hood, Wendy J.; and Goodman, Kenneth S. *Organizing for Whole Language.* Portsmouth, NH: Heinemann, 1991.

Graves, Donald. *Build a Literate Classroom.* Portsmouth, NH: Heinemann, 1991.

———. *A Researcher Learns to Write.* Portsmouth, NH: Heinemann, 1984.

Haack, Pam, and Merrilees, Cynthia. *Ten Ways to Become a Better Reader.* Cleveland, OH: Modern Curriculum Press, 1991.

———. *Write on Target.* Peterborough, NH: The Society For Developmental Education, 1991.

Hall, Nigel, and Robertson, Anne. *Some Day You Will No All About Me: Young Children's Explorations in the World of Letters.* Portsmouth, NH: Heinemann, 1991.

Holdaway, Don. *The Foundations of Literacy.* New York: Scholastic, 1979.

———. *Stability and Change in Literacy Learning.* Portsmouth, NH: Heinemann, 1984.

Pavelka, Patricia. *Making the Connection: Learning Skills Through Literature.* Peterborough, NH: Crystal Springs Books, 1995.

Peetboom, Adrian. *Shared Reading: Safe Risks with Whole Books.* Toronto, Ont.: Scholastic TAB, 1986.

Raines, Shirley C., and Canady, Robert J. *Story Stretchers.* Mt. Ranier, MD: Gryphon House, 1989.

———. *More Story Stretchers.* Mt. Ranier, MD: Gryphon House, 1991.

———. *Story Stretchers for the Primary Grades.* Mt. Ranier, MD: Gryphon House, 1992.

Rief, Linda. *Seeking Diversity: Language Arts with Adolescents.* Portsmouth, NH: Heinemann, 1992.

Routman, Regie. *Literacy at the Crossroads: Crucial Talk About Reading, Writing and Other Teaching Dilemmas.* Portsmouth, NH: Heinemann, 1996.

———. *Invitations: Changing as Teachers and Learners K-12.* Portsmouth, NH: Heinemann, 1991.

———. *Transitions: From Literature to Literacy.* Portsmouth, NH: Heinemann, 1988.

Vail, Priscilla. *Common Ground: Whole Language and Phonics Working Together.* Rosemont, NJ: Programs for Education, 1991.

Language Arts — Bilingual

Whitmore, Kathryn F., and Crowell, Caryl G. *Inventing a Classroom: Life in a Bilingual, Whole Language Learning Community.* York, ME: Stenhouse Publishers, 1994.

Language Arts — Spelling and Phonics

Bean, Wendy, and Bouffler, Christine. *Spell by Writing.* Portsmouth, NH: Heinemann, 1988.

Bolton, Faye, and Snowball, Diane. *Ideas for Spelling.* Portsmouth, NH: Heinemann, 1993.

Booth, David. *Spelling Links.* Ontario: Pembroke Publishers, 1991.

Buchanan, Ethel. *Spelling for Whole Language Classrooms*. Winnipeg, Man.: The C.E.L. Group, 1989.

Fry, Edward, Ph.D. *1000 Instant Words*. Laguna Beach, CA: Laguna Beach Educational Books, 1994.

————. *Phonics Patterns: Onset and Rhyme Word Lists*. Laguna Beach Educational Books, 1994.

Gentry, J. Richard. *My Kid Can't Spell*. Portsmouth, NH: Heinemann, 1996.

————. *Spel . . . Is a Four-Letter Word*. New York: Scholastic, 1987.

Gentry, J. Richard, and Gillet, Jean Wallace. *Teaching Kids to Spell*. Portsmouth, NH: Heinemann, 1993.

Lacey, Cheryl. *Moving on in Spelling: Strategies and Activities for the Whole Language Classroom*. New York: Scholastic, 1994.

Powell, Debbie, and Hornsby, David. *Learning Phonics and Spelling in a Whole Language Classroom*. New York: Scholastic, 1993.

Trisler, Alana, and Cardiel, Patrice. *My Word Book*. Rosemont, NJ: Modern Learning Press, 1994.

————. *Words I Use When I Write*. Rosemont, NJ: Modern Learning Press, 1989.

————. *More Words I Use When I Write*. Rosemont, NJ: Modern Learning Press, 1990.

Wagstaff, Janiel. *Phonics That Work! New Strategies for the Reading/Writing Classroom*. New York: Scholastic, 1995.

Wittels, Harriet, and Greisman, Joan. *How to Spell It*. New York: Putnam, 1982.

Learning Centers

Cook, Carole. *Math Learning Centers for the Primary Grades*. West Nynack, NY: The Center for Applied Research, 1992.

Ingraham, Phoebe Bell. *Creating and Managing Learning Centers: A Thematic Approach*. Peterborough, NH: Crystal Springs Books, Fall, 1996.

Isbell, Rebecca. *The Complete Learning Center Book*. Beltsville, MD: Gryphon House, 1995.

Poppe, Carol A., and Van Matre, Nancy A. *Language Arts Learning Centers for the Primary Grades*. West Nynack, NY: The Center for Applied Research in Education, 1991.

————. *Science Learning Centers for the Primary Grades*. West Nynack, NY: The Center for Applied Research in Education, 1985.

Wait, Shirleen S. *Reading Learning Centers for the Primary Grades*. West Nynack, NY: The Center for Applied Research, 1992.

Waynant, Louise, and Wilson, Robert M. *Learning Centers: A Guide for Effective Use*. Paoli, PA: Instructo Corp., 1974.

Learning Styles/Multiple Intelligences

Armstrong, Thomas. *In Their Own Way: Discovering and Encouraging Your Child's Personal Learning Style*. New York: Putnam, 1987.

————. *Learning Styles: Food for Thought and 130 Practical Tips for Teachers K-4*. Rosemont, NJ: Modern Learning Press, 1992.

————. *Multiple Intelligences in the Classroom*. Alexandria, VA: Association for Supervision and Curriculum Development, 1994.

———. *Seven Kinds of Smart: Identifying and Developing Your Many Intelligences*. New York: A Plume Book, 1993.

Banks, Janet Caudill. *Creative Projects for Independent Learners*. CATS Publications, 1995.

Bloom, Benjamin S. *All Our Children Learning: A Primer for Teachers and Other Educators*. New York: McGraw-Hill, 1981.

———, ed. *Developing Talent in Young People*. New York: Ballantine, 1985.

Campbell, Bruce. *The Multiple Intelligences Handbook: Lesson Plans and More . . . .* Stanwood, WA: Campbell & Associates, 1994.

Campbell, Linda; Campbell, Bruce; and Dickinson, Dee. *Teaching & Learning Through Multiple Intelligences*. Needham Heights, MA: Allyn & Bacon, 1996.

Carbo, Marie. *Reading Styles Inventory Manual*. Roslyn Heights, New York: National Reading Styles Institute, 1991.

Carbo, Marie; Dunn, Rita; and Dunn, Kenneth. *Teaching Students to Read Through Their Individual Learning Styles*. Needham Heights, MA: Allyn & Bacon, 1991.

Gardner, Howard. *Frames of Mind: The Theory of Multiple Intelligences*. New York: Basic Books, 1985.

———. *Multiple Intelligences: The Theory in Practice*. New York: Basic Books, 1990.

———. *The Unschooled Mind: How Children Think and How Schools Should Teach*. New York: Basic Books, 1990.

Gilbert, Labritta. *Do Touch: Instant, Easy Hands-on Learning Experiences for Young Children*. Mt. Ranier, MD: Gryphon House, 1989.

Grant, Janet Millar. *Shake, Rattle and Learn: Classroom-Tested Ideas That Use Movement for Active Learning*. York, ME: Stenhouse Publishers, 1995.

Lazear, David. *Multiple Intelligence Approaches to Assessment: Solving the Assessment Conundrum*. IRI/Skylight Publishing, Inc., 1994.

———. *Seven Pathways of Learning: Teaching Students and Parents About Multiple Intelligences*. Tucson, AZ: Zephyr Press, 1994.

———. *Seven Ways of Knowing: Teaching for Multiple Intelligences*. Palatine, IL: IRI/Skylight Publishing, Inc., 1991.

———. *Seven Ways of Teaching: The Artistry of Teaching With Multiple Intelligences*. Palatine, IL: IRI/Skylight Publishing, Inc., 1991.

New City School Faculty. *Celebrating Multiple Intelligences: Teaching for Success*. St. Louis, MO: The New City School, Inc., 1994.

Vail, Priscilla. *Gifted, Precocious, or Just Plain Smart*. Rosemont, NJ: Programs for Education, 1987.

———. *Learning Styles: Food for Thought and 130 Practical Tips for Teachers K-4*. Rosemont, NJ: Modern Learning Press, 1992.

Multiage Education

American Association of School Administrators. *The Nongraded Primary: Making Schools Fit Children*. Arlington, VA, 1992.

Anderson, Robert H., and Pavan, Barbara Nelson. *Nongradedness: Helping It to Happen*. Lancaster, PA: Technomic Press, 1992.

Banks, Janet Caudill. *Creating the Multi-age Classroom*. Edmonds, WA: CATS Publications, 1995.

Bingham, Anne A.; Dorta, Peggy; McClasky, Molly; and O'Keefe, Justine. *Exploring the Multiage Classroom*. York, ME: Stenhouse Publishers, 1995.

Davies, Anne; Politano, Colleen; and Gregory, Kathleen. *Together is Better*. Winnipeg, Canada: Peguis Publishers, 1993.

Gaustad, Joan. *"Making the Transition From Graded to Nongraded Primary Education."* Oregon School Study Council Bulletin, 35(8), 1992.

———. *"Nongraded Education: Mixed-Age, Integrated and Developmentally Appropriate Education for Primary Children."* Oregon School Study Council Bulletin, 35(7), 1992.

———. *"Nongraded Education: Overcoming Obstacles to Implementing the Multiage Classroom."* 38(3,4) Oregon School Study Council Bulletin, 1994.

Goodlad, John I., and Anderson, Robert H. *The Nongraded Elementary School*. New York: Teachers College Press, 1987. 248 pages.

Grant, Jim, and Johnson, Bob. *A Common Sense Guide to Multiage Practices*. Columbus, OH: Teachers' Publishing Group, 1995.

Grant, Jim; Johnson, Bob; and Richardson, Irv. *Multiage Q&A: 101 Practical Answers to Your Most Pressing Questions*. Peterborough, NH: Crystal Springs Books, 1995.

———. *Our Best Advice: The Multiage Problem Solving Handbook*. Peterborough, NH: Crystal Springs Books, 1996.

Grant, Jim, and Richardson, Irv, compilers. *Multiage Handbook: A Comprehensive Resource for Multiage Practices*. Peterborough, NH: Crystal Springs Books, 1996.

Maeda, Bev. *The Multi-Age Classroom*. Cypress, CA: Creative Teaching Press, 1994.

Miller, Bruce A. *Children at the Center: Implementing the Multiage Classroom*. Portland, OR: Northwest Regional Educational Laboratory; 1994.

———. *The Multigrade Classroom: A Resource Handbook for Small, Rural Schools*. Portland, OR: Northwest Regional Educational Laboratory, 1989.

———. *Training Guide for the Multigrade Classroom: A Resource for Small, Rural Schools*. Portland, OR: Northwest Regional Laboratory, 1990.

Ostrow, Jill. *A Room With a Different View: First Through Third Graders Build Community and Create Curriculum*. York, ME: Stenhouse Publishers, 1995.

Politano, Colleen, and Davies, Anne. *Multi-Age and More*. Winnipeg, Canada: Peguis Publishers, 1994.

Rathbone, Charles; Bingham, Anne; Dorta, Peggy; McClaskey, Molly; and O'Keefe, Justine. *Multiage Portraits: Teaching and Learning in Mixed-age Classrooms*. Peterborough, NH: Crystal Springs Books, 1993.

Virginia Education Association and Appalachia Educational Laboratory. *Teaching Combined Grade Classes: Real Problems and Promising Practices*. Charleston, WV: Appalachian Educational Laboratory, 1990.

Parent Involvement/Resources for Parents

Baskwill, Jane. *Parents and Teachers: Partners in Learning*. Toronto, Ont.: Scholastic, 1990.

Bettelheim, Bruno. *A Good Enough Parent*. New York: Alfred A. Knopf, 1987.

Butler, Dorothy, and Clay, Marie. *Reading Begins at Home*. Portsmouth, NH: Heinemann, 1982.

Clay, Marie. *Writing Begins at Home.* Portsmouth, NH: Heinemann, 1988.

Coletta, Anthony. *Kindergarten Readiness Checklist for Parents.* Rosemont, NJ: Modern Learning Press, 1991.

Elovson, Allanna. *The Kindergarten Survival Handbook.* Santa Monica, CA: Parent Ed Resources, 1991.

Grant, Jim. *Jim Grant's Book of Parent Pages.* Rosemont, NJ: Programs for Education, 1988.

Grant, Jim, and Azen, Margot. *Every Parent's Owner's Manuals. (Three-, Four-, Five-, Six-, Seven-Year-Old).* Rosemont, NJ: Programs for Education. 16 pages each manual.

Henderson, Anne T.; Marburger, Carl L.; and Ooms, Theodora. *Beyond the Bake Sale: An Educator's Guide to Working with Parents.* Columbia, MD: National Committee for Citizens in Education, 1990.

Hill, Mary. *Home: Where Reading and Writing Begin.* Portsmouth, NH: Heinemann, 1995.

Karnofsky, Florence, and Weiss, Trudy. *How to Prepare Your Child for Kindergarten.* Carthage, IL: Fearon Teacher Aids, 1993.

Lazear, David. *Seven Pathways of Learning: Teaching Students and Parents About Multiple Intelligences.* Tucson, AZ: Zephyr Press, 1994.

Lyons, P.; Robbins, A.; and Smith, A. *Involving Parents: A Handbook for Participation in Schools.* Ypsilanti, MI: High/Scope Press, 1984.

Vopat, James. *The Parent Project: A Workshop Approach to Parent Involvement.* York, ME: Stenhouse Publishers, 1994. 191 pages.

Themes

Atwood, Ron, ed. *Elementary Science Themes: Change Over Time; Patterns; Systems and Interactions; Models and Scales.* Lexington, KY: Institute on Education Reform, University of Kentucky, 1993. Set of four pamphlets, 50 pages each.

Bromley, Karen; Irwin-De Vitis, Linda; and Modlo, Marcia. *Graphic Organizers: Visual Strategies for Active Learning.* New York: Scholastic, 1995.

Davies, Anne; Politano, Colleen; and Cameron, Caren. *Making Themes Work.* Winnipeg, Canada: Peguis Publishers, 1993.

Gamberg, Ruth; Kwak, W.; Hutchins, R.; and Altheim, J. *Learning and Loving It: Theme Studies in the Classroom.* Portsmouth, NH: Heinemann, 1988.

Haraway, Fran, and Geldersma, Barbara. *12 Totally Terrific Theme Units.* New York: Scholastic, 1993.

Herr, Judy, and Libby, Yvonne. *Creative Resources for the Early Childhood Classroom.* Albany, NY: Delmar, 1990.

Katz, Lilian G., and Chard, Sylvia C. *Engaging Children's Minds: The Project Approach.* Norwood, NJ: Ablex Press, 1989.

McCarthy, Tara. *150 Thematic Writing Activities.* New York: Scholastic, 1993.

McCracken, Marlene and Robert. *Themes.* (9 book series). Winnipeg, Man.: Peguis, 1984-87.

SchifferDanoff, Valerie. *The Scholastic Integrated Language Arts Resource Book.* New York: Scholastic, 1995.

Schlosser, Kristin. *Thematic Units for Kindergarten.* New York: Scholastic, 1994.

Strube, Penny. *Theme Studies, A Practical Guide: How to Develop Theme Studies to Fit Your Curriculum.* New York: Scholastic, 1993.

Thompson, Gare. *Teaching Through Themes.* New York: Scholastic, 1991.

Index

It's Easy to Bring Outstanding Looping Presentations to Your School

Customized Inservice Training, Consulting and Keynote Speaking

If you're interested in training for your staff on multiyear programs and curriculum, just a simple phone call can start a Society For Developmental Education speaker on his or her way to your school. We can customize a wide range of presentations to meet the specific inservice training needs of your team. From the philosophy and benefits of multiyear classrooms, to specific classroom management techniques, to the bridging of multiyear curriculum, we have speakers available to train your team.

SDE's customized training program also has presenters available for numerous other popular topics:

- ✓ Multiage Practices
- ✓ Thematic Instruction
- ✓ Learning Centers
- ✓ Inclusion
- ✓ Readiness
- ✓ Positive Discipline
- ✓ Assessment
- ✓ Reading and Writing
- ✓ Multiple Intelligences
- ✓ Hands-on Science
- ✓ ADD/ADHD
- ✓ Math
- ✓ Retention
- ✓ Struggling Learners

SDE presenters are veteran educators who have provided training for teachers all across the country. They have extensive experience in their areas of expertise; many of them are published authors.

We offer solutions. From program design to travel logistics, our customized training department can alleviate all of the headaches associated with producing a successful inservice — and they can do so at a surprisingly affordable cost.

Call our customized training specialist, Jen Cilley, at 1-800-924-9621 for more information on how to schedule an outstanding presentation for your team.

The Society For Developmental Education
Ten Sharon Road • PO Box 577 • Peterborough, NH 03458

Other Valuable Resources

 Video!

Classroom Strategies for "Gray-Area" Children
by Gretchen Goodman

Gretchen will show you simple tips, techniques and strategies to help you address the needs of gray-area children; those children who may not qualify for special needs assistance, but who need special instructional adaptations. **Includes:** Teaching strategies and techniques to bring math from an abstract to a concrete level • Classroom techniques for children with "invisible disabilities" • Simple instructional strategies that work for unmotivated learners. 60 min.
#4324LH $69.95

Inclusive Classrooms from A to Z: A Handbook for Educators
by Gretchen Goodman

A guide for primary educators who include differently-abled children in their regular classrooms. Alphabetically arranged — from A: Acceptance to Z: Zero rejection. Answers the most frequently-asked questions about inclusion. Includes ideas for getting started; checklists, teacher-tested activities, and tips to use with staff, children, and parents; help with the planning process. Reproducible pages. (K-3) 199 pp.
#3707LH $24.95

I Can Learn! Strategies and Activities for Gray-Area Children
by Gretchen Goodman

"Gray-area" children (also known as slow learners, at-risk students or the "tweeners") are often in danger of falling between the cracks in the regular classroom unless teachers make accommodations for their special needs. *I Can Learn!* includes hundreds of easy-to-implement, teacher-tested ideas for adapting math, reading, writing, handwriting, and spelling activities to fit students' particular learning needs. Behavior management strategies and general classroom adaptations are also included. (K-4) 170 pp.
#4602LH $19.95

Making the Connection: Learning Skills Through Literature
by Pat Pavelka

Children are more likely to "make the connection" between skills and real-life learning when skills are taught at appropriate developmental levels and in the context of their own reading and writing.

Pat Pavelka, a primary teacher for 16 years, shows how to plan appropriate lessons and literature extension activities for emerging, developing, and independent readers while helping them develop an appreciation for literature. Skills include: capitalization, character development, phonics, main idea, point of view, drawing conclusions – and more. (K-2) 135 pp.
#4622LH $17.95
(Making the Connection for grades 3-6 available fall '96)

Write On Target
by Cindy Merrilees and Pam Haack

A wealth of easily-implemented ideas to help generate student interest in writing and meet the needs of a wide range of learners. Experienced classroom teachers, Cindy and Pam, give suggestions for writing individual student books, whole-group big books, journals, and creative writing booklets. They also explain how they solved the most frequently encountered problems of students writing every day. (1-3) 63 pp.
#1120LH $8.95

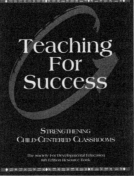

Teaching For Success
compiled by The Society For Developmental Education

The latest SDE Sourcebook has become a proven favorite with K-4 educators. It's packed with information about multiage, integrated curriculum, learning styles and multiple intelligences, inclusion, science, math and more. It includes reproducible pages you can use immediately in your classroom and a "teacher-friendly" resource listing. A must have. (K-4) 336 pp.
#4577LH $24.95

Creating Inclusive Classrooms: Education For All Children
compiled by The Society For Developmental Education

This resource book contains articles, resources, a bibliography, teacher-tested strategies and practices, and stories of schools that have successfully accommodated diverse learners in the regular classroom. Includes information on children who are "difficult or unusual," differently-abled, gray-area, cocaine-exposed, ADD, and learning disabled.
#3706LH $19.95

Shipping and Handling:

Up to $15.99	$3.85
$16.00 – 30.99	$4.75
$31.00 – 40.99	$5.85
$41.00 – 50.99	$6.75
$51.00 – 75.99	$7.95
$76.00 and over	10% of the Total Merchandise Price

FREE shipping and handling for orders over $250.

100% Satisfaction Guaranteed
Phone 1-800-321-0401

School Purchase Orders, Credit Cards and Personal Checks Accepted

MasterCard   VISA   DISCOVER

About the Authors

Jim Grant is an internationally known educator, consultant, and lecturer.

After serving as the teaching principal in a multiage school for almost two decades, he left to found The Society For Developmental Education, the nation's primary provider of staff development training through conferences, seminars, and customized inservice training, in the fields of developmental education, literacy, looping, multiage practices, and other related topics. He is also co-director of the National Alliance of Multiage Educators (N.A.M.E.) Grant is the author of several books, including *A Common Sense Guide to Multiage Practices* and *Multiage Q&A: 101 Practical Answers to Your Most Pressing Questions*, a compiler of the new *The Multiage Handbook: A Comprehensive Resource for Multiage Practices*, and the coauthor of *Our Best Advice: The Multiage Problem Solving Handbook*.

Jim has emerged as the nation's leading proponent of looping; in addition to this book, he has created two versions of a video, "The Looping Classroom." One version is for teachers and administrators, the other for parents.

Bob Johnson is a former teacher and principal of a system of five fully multiage schools.

For the past 20 years Johnson has conducted workshops, seminars, keynotes and inservices nationwide. He is a workshop leader, author, and lecturer, and serves as senior associate consultant with The Society For Developmental Education. He was instrumental in founding the National Alliance of Multiage Educators, and currently serves on the advisory board. He is coauthor, with Jim Grant and Irv Richardson, of *Multiage Q&A: 101 Practical Answers to Your Most Pressing Questions*, and *Our Best Advice: The Multiage Problem Solving Handbook*, and, with Jim Grant, of *A Common Sense Guide to Multiage Practices*.

Irv Richardson received the Maine Teacher of the Year Award in 1988 and the Maine Educator Award from the Milken Family Foundation in 1992.

After graduation from Dartmouth College, Richardson taught third grade at the Union-Sanborn school in Tilton, New Hampshire. He then moved to the Freeport Public School in Freeport, Maine, where he served as the teacher/ director of the elementary gifted and talented program, and as the teaching principal of a nongraded, multilevel program for seven-to-ten-year-olds at Mast Landing School. He has consulted and lectured on multiage education nationwide, and has taught graduate-level courses on multiage practices.

As Program Director for The Society For Developmental Education, Richardson oversees staff development conferences and inservice training throughout the United States. He is also co-director of the National Alliance of Multiage Educators. He is coauthor of *Multiage Q&A: 101 Practical Answers to Your Most Pressing Questions* and *Our Best Advice: The Multiage Problem Solving Handbook*, and the cocompiler of *The Multiage Handbook: A Comprehensive Resource for Multiage Practices*.